SHARING SHALOM

Studies in
Judaism and Christianity

*Exploration of Issues in the
Contemporary Dialogue Between
Christians and Jews*

Editor in Chief for
Stimulus Books
Helga Croner

Editors
Lawrence Boadt, C.S.P.
Helga Croner
Rabbi Leon Klenicki
Rev. Dr. John Koenig
Kevin A. Lynch, C.S.P.
Dennis McManus
Dr. Susan Shapiro

 A STIMULUS BOOK

SHARING SHALOM

A Process for Local Interfaith Dialogue between Christians and Jews

**Philip A. Cunningham
and
Arthur F. Starr
Editors**

A STIMULUS BOOK
PAULIST PRESS ◆ NEW YORK ◆ MAHWAH, N.J.

The Publisher gratefully acknowledges use of the following material: "Bashanah Habaah" by Ehud Manor. Copyright © Ehud Manor—ACUM—Israel. Reprinted by permission of ACUM, Tel Aviv, Israel. "Partners" from *Does God Have a Big Toe? Stories About Stories in the Bible,* by Marc Gellman. Copyright © 1989 by Marc Gellman. Reprinted by permission of HarperCollins Publishers, New York.

Cover design by John Murello.

Library of Congress Cataloging-in-Publication Data

Sharing Shalom : a process for local interfaith dialogue between Christians and Jews / [edited] by Philip A. Cunningham and Arthur F. Starr.
   p. cm—(Studies in Judaism and Christianity) (Stimulus book)
  Includes bibliographical references.
  ISBN 0–8091–3835–2 (alk. paper)
  1. Judaism—Relations—Christianity—Congresses. 2. Christianity and other religions—Judaism—Congresses. I. Cunningham, Philip A. II. Starr, Arthur F., 1942– . III. Series.
BM535.S35 1998
261.2′6—dc21   98–38566
                                                                  CIP

Published by Paulist Press
997 Macarthur Boulevard
Mahwah, New Jersey 07430

www.paulistpress.com

Printed and bound in the
United States of America

Contents

Appendix 3: For More Information

Acknowledgments

We would like to thank the following people who helped design the *Sharing Shalom* process or who helped improve it with the experience gained by hosting *Sharing Shalom* in their local communities:

Mr. Norman Abelson
Rabbi Herman Blumberg
Bro. Paul R. Demers, S.C.
Ms. Polly Dickson
Rev. William Donoghue
Rev. Edward Horstmann
Rev. Hays M. Junkin

Rev. Louise Mann
Rev. Dr. Philip J. Mayher
Ms. Joan Parrish
Ms. Joyce Pastor
Ms. Joan Poro
Ms. Judith Wolff

We would also like to thank Dr. Carol J. Descoteaux, C.S.C., president of Notre Dame College, for her sponsorship of the Shalom Center.

Finally, special gratitude is also extended to the Most Rev. Leo E. O'Neil, D.D., Bishop of the Catholic Diocese of Manchester, both for his personal support and for a generous grant that made possible the distribution of the first edition of the *Sharing Shalom Guidebook.*

Dedicated to the late

Leo E. O'Neil

Bishop of the Catholic Diocese of Manchester, New Hampshire

Foreword
Why Celebrate *Nostra Aetate*?

Most Rev. Leo E. O'Neil, Bishop of Manchester

[Editors' Note: In the last months of his life, the late Bishop of Manchester, Leo E. O'Neil, intended to adapt as a foreword for this book an address he had delivered at Temple Adath Yeshurun on the occasion of the thirtieth anniversary of the Second Vatican Council declaration Nostra Aetate. *We honor the memory of this good man by presenting that important address here. It has been edited slightly for this context based on conversations with him before his death. Readers will see glimpses of his poet's heart, his dry and often self-deprecating humor, and more important, encounter profound reasons why the interfaith dialogue between Jews and Christians is so important.]*

In 1970, I made a pilgrimage to Israel. Two priest friends and I arrived in Jerusalem on *Shabbat*. We were on our own, wanting to discover the city by ourselves. We had no guides, but armed with maps and with great confidence in our unfailing sense of direction, we knew we would arrive at the Western Wall of the Temple Mount by sundown.

So we thought! The ravages of war were still strewn everywhere in the city. We climbed over rubble, stumbled over the remains of buildings—and were hopelessly lost.

I happened to notice an old man, dressed all in black, lumbering along. I told the others that I was going to ask him to show us the way to the Wall. I was soundly ridiculed. How was he going to answer my question? Who would interpret his answer? I went ahead and asked the old man anyway. Staring at me with solemn intent, he simply said, "Come," and waved us on.

The journey went from bad to worse. We began to climb a steep hill, moving

1

away from the city. My friends' lack of trust mounted with each step—and so did their frustration with me. The old man silently led us up to an apartment complex, lumbered along some stairs, glancing back now and then to see if we were still following. He came to a door, unlocked it, motioned to us once more, and said, "Come." When we entered the apartment, he flung open the shutters and beckoned us to the window. Far below us was the Western Wall; the city, dazzled in a golden haze; hundreds of people, scurried to be in place to pray at sundown. It was a rare religious experience for all of us—a faith journey to the Holy City.

Why the old man never spoke on the way up the hill, I don't know. He knew English well. We told him we were three priests. He smiled and said, "Four priests. I am Cohen." Later he told us he was a maker of yarmulkes, and placed one on each of our heads as we stood looking down at the Temple Mount, hearing now, not the hubbub of city noise, but the murmur of Sabbath prayer drifting up the hill.

My visit to Israel was as personally awesome as my first visit to Ireland. Both times I was overwhelmed. Everywhere I looked I thought I recognized relatives. The brooding weather unsettled my soul, and that melancholic shadow that haunts every Irishman drew me into an almost mystical retreat. This feeling of returning to my roots, swirling me into my own spiritual struggles, profoundly affected me. It made me confront myself.

This feeling is renewed in my later visits to Jewish synagogues. Here I encounter my great relatives, Abraham, Sara, Isaac, Israel, Joseph, Jeremiah—some of whom have the same capacity as my own tribe to be at ease with God, tinged with a melancholic restlessness, and at the same time, always breathing new hope into human weariness.

Coming to Jewish houses of prayer, a man or woman walks into a hall of spiritual heroes—yet its walls echo human horror as well. Each of us must be prepared to discover once again his or her faith identity—an identity that can never be found apart from relationship to God, to our past, to each other.

These thoughts enfold me as I pose the question (a good rabbinical approach): "Why celebrate *Nostra Aetate*?"

First of all, perhaps we have to define what *Nostra Aetate* is. *Nostra Aetate* is a document of the Second Vatican Council. It defines, from the Catholic side, the relationship that must exist between the Roman Catholic Church and the Jewish community. It is a document that sets the course. It is a document that attempts to correct the sins of the past and establish the ground for continued growth in mutual understanding and theological dialogue. It is only the first of several documents of the Catholic Church and other Christian denominations that promote discussions with members of the Jewish faith. It is important to us because it challenges us to study and to reflect on our common origins and to examine the mutual bonding we have because we are a covenanted people.

I admit I was surprised when I discovered in the Latin dictionary the meaning of *celebrare* is "to visit often; to give honor." Our question then is: "Why visit *Nostra Aetate* again?" The *obvious* answer is that most of us have never done it. The *nagging* answer is that if we have, we have not moved quickly from words to action; and the *demanding* answer is that we look at some of the very simple, easily understood ideas present in this document and develop our own spirituality from them.

The document declares, "All peoples comprise a single community and have a single origin. One also is their final goal—God. His manifestations of goodness and saving designs extend to all."

These ideas are derived from both the Jewish and Christian Scriptures and are now the text of *Nostra Aetate,* one of the shortest, but also one of the fundamental declarations of the historic Second Vatican Council. *Nostra Aetate* is a word symbol of conversion, calling us to a continuing change of heart.

Even the title is revealing: *Nostra Aetate*—"In Our Day." Scripture often uses "time" in ways different from the ways we do. The "time of Shabbat" is a manifestation of "divine time" in our ordinary lives and foretells a "time" to come. However, in another sense the time of God is inscrutable to us. It is God's prerogative to measure the days, the seasons in his own good time. But in our collective time since 1938 things are different. It is with this background that *Nostra Aetate* derives its spiritual dimension. We can never look at human history again without examining why a people were hounded, rounded up, loaded into freight trains, forced to labor and eventually cruelly martyred. Never before, or since, has the human person's body and spirit been tortured in such evil ways—nor the entire human family been responsible for an atrocity of such magnitude.

Such devastation demands conversion: a determination of the soul to assume proper guilt, seek personal and collective reconciliation, and radically change things "in our day."

No wonder some people assume God is dead. Words—his words—his living words given for the redemption and salvation of the human family were, and tragically, even now are used to destroy a people he himself has chosen. Even Christian liturgical prayers that contained words like "perfidious" fly in the face of the word destined to inspire hope but which, in fact, incited prejudice and deep-seated hatred. *Nostra Aetate* is not about "politically correct" language. It is about the absolute, eternal Word of God transcending every human limit and bringing us to the divine design of the Eternal One.

For this reason, the Second Vatican Council teaches: "The Jews should not be presented as repudiated or cursed by God as if such views followed from

Holy Scriptures. All should take pains, then, lest in catechetical instruction and in the preaching of God's Word they teach anything out of harmony with the truth of the Gospel and the spirit of Christ."

That is a good beginning. But it has absolutely no power unless we admit that, at times, we can be tempted to a theology that gives life to our prejudice. Moreover, a spirituality that begets conversion, a theological and scriptural awareness of the concept of covenant must anchor all of us. Unless we understand the covenant made with Israel; unless we appreciate the depth of fidelity to that covenant; unless we know the God, who with tremendous signs and wonders and even rainbows, pledged himself to Abraham, Isaac and Jacob, we can never understand the invitation of Jesus, whom Christians acknowledge as the Christ.

The permanency of the covenant with Abraham and Israel has steadily evolved in Christian thought since Vatican II. That progress enriches not so much the Jewish people as it does those who follow the Gospel of Jesus because it stretches our approach to God's divine intervention in the history of the entire human family. It is at once both universal and particular. It is ever new and yet rooted in the mists of Ur, the Sinai, Horeb, Eretz Israel.

To deny the permanency of the covenant is to doubt the Lord and his fidelity to his Word. God cannot deny himself. His eternal Word is immutable.

Pope John Paul II's plea, in October of 1995 at the United Nations General Assembly, "to make room for the mystery of God" is best understood in the light of the whole history of salvation. From the first question in the Bible, "Adam, where are you?" God constantly seeks to enter into dialogue with the human person. The covenant of Israel is the beginning of its story and it is the basis for the Christian's search "in our day" for meaning in the madness and chaos we see all around us.

Why celebrate *Nostra Aetate?* To see what we have done with its challenge. Anyone involved in education knows that negative teaching, despite its best efforts, is apt to produce negative results—many times what we least expect or want. The conciliar admonition, "should *not* be presented as repudiated or cursed by God," demands a *positive* expression. When we speak of Israel, there must be employed what Catholic theology calls the gifts of the Spirit: "awe and reverence." Israel heard God speak. God's spirit dwells in Israel. Israel wandered in faith for forty years with legitimate complaint and with even not so valid protests about things like cucumbers and garlic. But how many of us plague the Lord with similar gripes?

Israel repented; Israel lived the ambiguity of faith in exile and in hope. We Christians have much to learn. Our catechetical approach to Jewish studies should herald as well the wonderful, frustrating aspects of the church on pilgrimage, set against the background of Moses and his people trekking across the desert.

My limited experience with textbooks shows that we have made remarkable progress in instilling in our young people the power of Israel's witness of faith in the midst of doubt and confusion. Once, I was visiting one of our schools dressed in full liturgical robes, wearing a zucchetto. Surely, I thought, all our Catholic children know only a bishop wears such a hat. I just wanted them to say I was a bishop, and I had a wonderful homily to move on with. So I took the zucchetto off my head, held it in the air, and asked, "Who wears one of these?" The entire class shouted: "Jewish people!"

Unperturbed, I held my staff in hand. Now everyone, absolutely everyone, knows this is a symbol that the bishop is a shepherd. So I asked, "Why do I carry this?" One precocious youngster yelled: "Because you're old!"

In retrospect, I was thrilled at the first answer. Our students know and recognize symbols of other religions. (Although I admire the astuteness of the second response, I am appalled that we allow such a lack of diplomacy in our schools.)

We need to keep alive ancient symbols, but we must heed the plea of the present. Pope John Paul II constantly urges us to respect the dignity of every human person. His call is the power of *Nostra Aetate,* propelling us into the future. It is a challenge for Christians that is rooted in Christ, who calls us to seek first the kingdom of God by living the great prayer of Israel, the Shema: "Hear, O Israel! The Lord is our God, the Lord alone!"

Sometimes, it seems we have simply failed in our day—genocide in Bosnia and Cambodia; one tribe against another in Africa; the subtle prejudice; the fear; xenophobia—will they ever defeat us? Never! Look to the sons and daughters of Israel! In the face of all this they triumphed, and they will triumph again.

The Catholic Church has developed an extraordinary theology of social justice. She has witnessed proudly to this theology in her institutions. Every aspect that affects the quality of life of the human person she has tried to protect and serve. Once, in the recent past, she was largely silent; now, she cries out for justice. She serves the poor and the outcast and defends all human rights. But we Catholic Christians have failed to make social justice an intimate part of our life of prayer. Our teaching of social justice has its roots in the prophetic voice of the Jewish tradition. It must be a part of our spiritual life. It must be integrated into the way we think and act.

We have been taught, and are being warned, that we must respect the dignity of every person—friend and stranger, and even enemy. To turn aside from that tradition is a betrayal of the faith of our ancestors.

Why do I, a Catholic bishop, look to Jews? What strength do I find in their continuing covenant with God?

> Enrich my soul with your theology of exile.
> Let me understand I have no lasting home here.
> Teach me to yearn for the courts of the Lord.
> Remind me that life is a pilgrimage, sometimes a trek across a hostile desert.

As I walk through dark valleys, help me to "Lift up my eyes to the mountains from whence my help shall come."

Stretch my being to pray—pleading, even bargaining with God as Abraham did. Make every mood of my soul and emotion sing with David's psalms. Let me be as restless as the prophet with the urgency of God.

With Micah, make me the voice of the poor—to love tenderly, to act with justice, to walk humbly with my God. Fire me with rage against any injustice. Make me a prophetic voice. Give me courage to risk for the *anawim,* the poor, of God.

Challenge me to be sabbath; to seek silence, listening to the whisper of God calling in the night wind and in all of the events of the human experience. Demand that I make room for the mystery of God in my life and in our common life together.

Make me a Jonah, a sign of resurrection and hope.

Why celebrate *Nostra Aetate?* Because it makes me know my ancestry and my destiny. I am a Catholic. I love my faith; and I love the Jews because they preserve for me the image, the words of the one God who is "rich in mercy and abounding kindness."

We celebrate *Nostra Aetate* to eradicate all hatred and prejudice by our teaching, our writing, our preaching and our acting. The Shoah is not an historic event come and gone. It is a living affront to God and an insult to every human person. We must live with that every day. If we don't, then we will forget and, in our forgetting, give excuse for other horrible ovens and gas chambers to appear.

The Holocaust is a living memorial to a culture of death that can only be conquered by a living faith, a living covenant. And despite the millions consumed in the Shoah, perhaps because of them, the Shema is still proclaimed. And it is only because of the Shema that, for Christians, the Gospel can make any sense.

I wonder if the proper description of the Jews who were killed in the terrible Holocaust might be martyrs rather than simply victims. True, they had no control over their fate, but they gave more than passive resistance. They died simply because they were Jews. Our souls shudder at how often the words

> Out of the depths I cry to you, O Lord;
> Lord, hear my voice!
> Let your ears be attentive
> to the voice of my pleading,

echoed in those death chambers.

It would be right and just and proper to our salvation to commemorate every year, in our sacred liturgy, prayer in memory of the martyrs who perished in those infamous camps, so that we could keep alive the horror of this human catastrophe.

We have work to do! In 1995 Jews and Christians gathered to inaugurate the Shalom Center at Notre Dame College, an ambitious but necessary institute. It is a practical way of implementing the hopes and dreams of hundreds of believers of all faiths. I was happy to offer assistance in the printing of the Center's curriculum for local interfaith dialogue between Jews and Christians and am gratified that this work is now being published for wider use. Jews and Christians must learn to talk about their faith with each other. This work of building spiritual solidarity between Christians and Jews is a project of great hope but, I am sure, fraught with many difficulties.

In my office there is a framed quotation from 1 Chronicles. It is my daily challenge and consolation. I offer it as a prayer for the work of Jewish and Christian reconciliation and partnership.

> Don't be frightened by the size of the task.
> Be strong and courageous and get to work.
> For the Lord my God is with you.
> He will not forsake you.
> He will see to it that everything is finished correctly.

Let us, like Abraham, set out in faith, believing God's fidelity will show us a place along the way.

Foreword

Rabbi Leon Klenicki
Director, Department of Interfaith Affairs
of the Anti-Defamation League of B'nai B'rith

Martin Buber said in 1936, a time of great pain for German Jews under the domination of the Hitlerian totalitarian system, that "no person outside Israel knows the mystery of Israel. And no person outside of Christianity knows the mystery of Christianity. But in their ignorance they can acknowledge each other in the mystery." Buber's thoughts and hope became a reality after the Second World War and especially in the fifties and sixties. The Roman Catholic Church and other Christian denominations, after the impact of the total horror of the Holocaust, an infamous event that occurred in the very heart of Christianity, started reckoning with the meaning of Judaism and the Christian-Jewish relationship. This reckoning attempts to understand the meaning of the God-Israel covenant despite hundreds of years of teaching contempt toward Judaism. The Second Vatican Council and bodies of other Christian churches issued documents on the meaning of the Christian-Jewish encounter. The *Nostra Aetate* declaration, promulgated on October 20, 1965, marked a special moment in the history of the Church and its relation to world religions, especially Judaism and the Jewish people. It opened the doors to a dialogue encounter, overcoming a millennium of monologues. Dialogue became a reality in some countries, especially in the United States, where the meeting of Jews and Christians fostered the social exchange, as well as a respectful acceptance of the other person of faith.

The days of tolerance, the product of the French and Industrial Revolutions in Europe, are succeeded in our days by a new form of community relationship. It is no longer the toleration of the other person of faith, but rather the acceptance of the other person in God, for God. The *aggiornamento* initiated by the Second Vatican Council and other Christian denominations was a process of inner renewal entailing a reckoning of the soul in relation to other faith commitments. The Council, in particular, undertook a rethinking of Judaism and the Jewish people in Catholic theology. Negative Christian attitudes of centuries, the teaching of contempt, the denial of Israel's destiny and vocation, required a reflection going beyond the theological triumphalism of the Church Fathers and the ideas of medieval Catholic theologians.

In October 1974, Pope Paul VI established in the Vatican a Commission for Religious Relations with the Jews, which in 1975 issued the *Guidelines and Suggestions for Implementing the Conciliar Declaration* Nostra Aetate (No. 4). This document suggested changes in the approach to liturgy, teaching and education, and joint social action. The document was an advance over *Nostra Aetate,* but not in relation to previously published guidelines of the Catholic Episcopal Conferences in the United States and Europe. A third document was issued in 1985, *Notes on the Correct Way to Present Jews and Judaism in Preaching and Catechesis in the Roman Catholic Church.*

The Vatican documents were an invitation for Christians and Jews to dialogue. It has been done in general at high levels of the Vatican and national episcopal conferences, but in a few cases it has taken a popular dimension. The exchange between the Jewish and Catholic communities of New Hampshire and Massachusetts through *Sharing Shalom* is a good example of an I-Thou relationship. I was happy to be a participant at the launch of the Shalom Center's activities in Manchester, New Hampshire, in 1995. At that time, the thirty years since *Nostra Aetate* were celebrated by founding a center dedicated to promoting an I-Thou relationship between Christians and Jews. I also recognized the late Bishop Leo O'Neil's strong endorsement and support of this mission as yet another sign of the church's ongoing commitment to dialogue with Judaism.

Dr. Philip A. Cunningham and Rabbi Arthur F. Starr are to be congratulated for editing this book, as well as for their daily work of implementing the dialogue at pew levels. This book reflects the concerns of both Jews and Christians about their heritage and their relationship to local communities and the nation. The different articles reflect social concerns, but also open the possibility of a theological exchange that should nurture the interfaith dialogue.

The Jewish participants in the *Sharing Shalom* experience have overcome a difficult matter for the Jews. Theological discussions or conversations bring back memories of other times when Jews were confronted theologically. Rabbis and teachers were asked to explain biblical texts that, according to Christian theologians, referred to Jesus and his vocation. The medieval "theological conversations" ended with the Jews being expelled from a city or converted by force. The Christian theological triumphalism presented Jews as a deicide people without any role in God's design. It was the teaching of contempt that was reflected for centuries in art, literature, and, most especially, preaching. This is not the reality that the authors share with their fellow friends, Christian or Jewish, in *Sharing Shalom.* They share the meaning of the spiritualities, as well as their beliefs. What does it mean to be Jewish or what does it mean to be Christian? The significance of the Shabbat celebration or the Christian Sunday worship, the question of the Messiah in Judaism and Christianity, and a joint reflection on the two thousand years of being together in the world are all explored in its pages.

The Christian-Jewish dialogue is a recent and very unique phenomenon. For centuries, Christians and Jews have been relating in an interchange of monologues, each community defending or attacking, but never sharing their feeling of God, the presence of God in their midst. *Sharing Shalom,* however, is *sharing.* This is the contribution of this book. It might not change the world at this moment, but it will contribute to a better understanding of each other by making available the special encounter of Christians and Jews through the Shalom Center. The studies and the conversations among the Christian and Jewish participants are an invitation to look at each other as part of the people of God. Both communities recognize God as the very essence of their life. The exchange is a process of sharing with the other person of faith the intimacy of the God-person relationship.

The editors and participants have followed a thought that is present in the work of the Jewish-French philosopher Emmanuel Levinas. In one of his books, he said that "the existence of God is sacred history itself, the sacredness of man's relation to man through which God may pass." Levinas points out the need to look at each other as subjects of faith. His is an invitation to look at the other person, at his face, as a person of God, where the divine inspiration is reflected. In a real I-Thou encounter, we see the other person as a person of God, not a subject of contempt or an object in itself. The Spanish philosopher Jose Ortega Gassett defined a totalitarian system or any system of triumphalism as "cosification." This is to make an object, *la cosa,* of a person of flesh and blood, created by God, inspired in his or her life by God's commands and witnessing the covenantal relationship in the private life and the life of the community. *Sharing Shalom* reflects this attempt to overcome the sense of looking at another person as an object, sharing with a fellow person a feeling of obligation and responsibility. To accept the other person of faith is to be responsible for that person. *Sharing Shalom* follows this line of bringing the peace of the heart, making the other person part of the community of faith.

The word *shalom* in Hebrew is a way of greeting of each other, but it also projects another dimension. Shalom relates to *shalem,* "to be completed." Perhaps the very choice of the word *shalom* by the editors projects this message of completeness in the relationship of Jews and Christians. It is a completeness as people of God, though each community is committed to its particular faith commitment. It is not an invitation to the conversion of one group to the religion of the other, but rather a conversion of the heart, accepting the other person as a person of God, a subject of faith, not an object of contempt. This is indeed the great contribution of *Sharing Shalom,* and we are grateful to the editors and participants for their creation. May God bless them for their work.

Introduction

In January of 1994 a group of about thirty Jews and Christians from the greater Manchester, New Hampshire, area traveled together on a ten-day interfaith study tour to Israel. Included in the group were congregants from local synagogues and churches, college professors and students, and Christian and Jewish clergy. The experience was so profound that the group's leaders resolved to institute some formal structure to continue and promote increased understanding between Jews and Christians. Thus was born the Shalom Center at Notre Dame College.

Established at a Catholic liberal arts college with a strong commitment to the local community, the Shalom Center saw that it could play a key role in implementing the recommendation of the National Conference of Catholic Bishops that Christian-Jewish relations "should be advanced on all levels...[including] at the popular level...." ("Guidelines for Catholic-Jewish Relations" [1967], Recommended Programs 1 and 6). It was decided to prepare a multiweek curricular process to enable local interfaith dialogue at multiple sites through the state and region.

The programs committee of the Shalom Center set to work. Topics were selected to be the focus of conversations that would occur during six weekly gatherings. To set the stage for these dialogues, Jews and Christians were invited to write short personal, reflective essays on each topic. These essays would be read in advance by participants, who would then come together to discuss the topics by means of reflection questions and under the guidance of a small-group facilitator. The curriculum which developed was entitled *Sharing Shalom*. Thanks to a grant from Bishop Leo O'Neil of the Diocese of Manchester, guidebooks were photocopied for distribution to everyone who participated in the process.

In 1996–97, *Sharing Shalom* occurred in five sites throughout the area: in Exeter, Hopkinton, Manchester and Nashua, New Hampshire, and in Weston, Massachusetts. These programs were made possible through the generosity and dedication of leaders in those communities who felt it was important to do

13

the work of inviting people, setting up schedules and meeting spaces, and hosting the sessions. The experience gained by these events has shaped the revised curriculum that you now are reading.

It is our hope that the publication of our efforts will encourage other Christians and Jews to learn from one another and thereby share God's shalom within their communities.

Welcome to Participants

It gives us great pleasure to welcome you to this six-week process in which Jews and Christians can come together to begin to foster greater understanding and mutual esteem. The Shalom Center has designed this process so that:

1. Participants can learn about one another by sharing personal experiences;
2. Common misperceptions and stereotypes about the other can be dispelled;
3. Interfaith respect and friendship might develop;
4. Common prayer to the One with whom both Jews and Christians are in covenant can be experienced;
5. Participants might be inspired to work together to promote the common good.

This guidebook will help the process to unfold by introducing the general topics to be discussed for each of the six weeks. As part of your commitment to *Sharing Shalom,* consistency of attendance is important. The dynamics within your small group will be noticeably affected if the participants vary from week to week. You are also expected to read weekly essays, written by Jews and Christians, expressing their own personal perspectives on each week's subject. The essays are written by people with varying educational and career backgrounds. Some are theologians or clergy; others pursue different careers. They also represent some of the different denominations and movements within their religious heritages. All are committed to dialogue and collaboration between Christians and Jews. Following each week's essays are reflection/discussion questions to think about before you gather for interfaith dialogue. At the dialogue, your small-group facilitator will guide you in sharing ideas or questions that the essays may have raised in your mind.

Depending on the options selected by your program sponsors, each week may open with a specially prepared exercise to launch the conversation and may end with a prayer in which both Jews and Christians can readily join. The heart of the *Sharing Shalom* process, however, is the opportunity to dialogue freely with people from a different, though related, religious tradition. We believe that you will learn as much about your own faith as you will about the heritage of your conversation partners.

Here are some commonsense principles to observe as you get to know your dialogue partners and converse about one another's faith tradition:

1. Enter into dialogue so that *you* can learn and grow; not to change the other.
2. Be conscious of the need to allow people the space to enter the discussion. Some people are more sheepish about offering their thoughts, but will be encouraged to do so if more outspoken persons avoid dominating the exchange.
3. Everyone must be honest and sincere, even if that means revealing discomforts with your own tradition or that of the other. Everyone must assume that everyone else is being equally honest and sincere.
4. Everyone must be permitted to define their own religious experience and identity, and this must be respected by others.
5. Don't feel that you are the spokesperson for your entire faith tradition or that you ought somehow to know everything there is to know about it. Admit any confusion or uncertainty you might have if a puzzling question arises.
6. Don't assume in advance where points of agreement or disagreement will exist.
7. Everyone should be willing to be self-critical.
8. All should strive to experience the other's faith "from within" and be prepared to view themselves differently as a result of an "outside" perspective.
9. Trust is a must.

Adapted from Leonard Swidler, "The Dialogue Decalogue," *Journal of Ecumenical Studies* 20/1:1–4.

SESSION ONE

What Being a Jew Means to Me

David G. Stahl

To be a Jew in American society is to remain in many ways an outsider. The fact of birth to a Jewish mother (the traditional rabbinic test of Jewishness) is, for most Jews today, a setting apart from the mainstream of American society.

Start, then, with birth. I was born to Jewish parents and brought up in a moderately traditional Jewish environment. I was fortunate to know two sets of grandparents (and one pair of great-grandparents, though only marginally). But I did come from a tradition of observance and also of study. My grandparents were fairly learned in Jewish customs (both religious and cultural) and imparted some of it to me. My parents were less learned than their own parents but still bound to a tradition that they felt strongly. My own religious schooling (four afternoons each week after regular school) lasted for a number of years, but I found that it did not answer many of my questions.

Only as an adult did I come to know more of the cultural context of Judaism and reach the conviction that Jewish teaching and belief had become, willy-nilly, a large part of the fabric of my consciousness. I had learned to view my own situation as being outside the context of most Americans, imbued with a sense of otherness, yet sure that what I once saw as a kind of separation had enormous validity for me.

A learned rabbi once, when asked to sum up Jewish belief while standing on one foot, replied, "Do not do to another what you would not want done to yourself. All the rest is commentary. Now go and study." That same idea, of course, is embodied in the golden rule of Christian teaching.

I have learned, mostly as an adult, some of the great messages Judaism has to offer the world. First and foremost is the obligation of justice for one's fellow man. Judaism teaches that Jews have an obligation to apply standards of fairness and decency in their relations with their coworkers, their neighbors, the people with whom they interact, whether Jew or non-Jew. Judaism teaches that everyone has an obligation of charity for others. Even the Hebrew term *tzedakah,* generally translated as "charity," really means "righteousness."

Judaism teaches the obligation to study and to learn. All one need do is to enumerate the contributions made by Jews to science, to literature, to law, to recognize the impact of Jewish teaching on the Jewish people. These principles have seemed to me a great guide to living, worthy of being passed on to future generations.

Judaism emphasizes, too, that human nature is social. While placing an obligation on the individual for his or her own behavior, Jewish practice also requires participation in a group. A Jewish service must have ten adults for the recitation of congregational prayers, but does not require a rabbi.

As an adult, I have also come to recognize and to appreciate the variety of expression that Jewish ideas and ideals have taken. Once the aim of Jewish study was only to be steeped in religious lore. Over time, Jewish scholarship has come to recognize all knowledge as valid and worthy of study.

If it were only ethical teaching that defined Judaism, it could be argued that certainly Christian beliefs derive from Jewish concepts and teach the same ethical practices. Then why preserve the separations that define Judaism? For me, that question only goes back to the original premise. I am Jewish because I was born to Jewish parents and raised in an environment that taught Jewish history, customs and practices. Those facts are, for me, a validation of my own beliefs.

I like the culture I come from. It is diverse yet unified. I have learned that being Jewish involves asking hard questions and seeking answers that may not always be obvious. Most people who consider themselves Jewish share many aspects of this culture. From the Jewish devotion to study and debate comes the oft-repeated jest, "Two Jews, three opinions." I have learned to like this intellectual interplay with my fellows. Even among the ultra-Orthodox, who often project an aura of certainty, their teaching is also one of discussion, of worrying at problems, of seeking answers but still demonstrating willingness to live with the unanswerable. Judaism, as religious belief, is not easy. It requires much effort from the individual. But with Judaism comes a set of concepts which, I believe, provide a sound basis for a societal life.

What Being a Christian Means to Me

Louise Mann

For me, to be a Christian is to belong to a community of faith that proclaims the risen Jesus as Redeemer and Lord; a community that is confident, because of the resurrection of Jesus, that the world is being transformed into the kingdom of God. This is the "Good News" or "Gospel" that Christians declare.

Since the first century C.E., this community has evolved into a number of identifiable expressions, including the Anglican, Eastern Orthodox, Reformed, Congregational and Roman Catholic. I am a member of the Episcopal Church and so find myself within the Anglican stream of Christianity. This means that I am a member of a parish, Christ Church, which is part of a diocese, the Episcopal Diocese of New Hampshire, which is part of Province I (New England) of the Episcopal Church of the USA, which is affiliated with the other national churches of the Anglican Communion throughout the world.

At the same time, we are part of the ecumenical movement that seeks to focus on what various Christian bodies hold in common as well as valuing the diversity that expands all of our Christian horizons. We are also part of the movement among Christians that seeks to understand and value our particular relationship to Jewish people. This means a willingness to look carefully at the terrible history of Christian persecution of Jews and to work to make that history understood among Christians so that we can move toward a very different and much more positive relationship in the present and for the future. It includes active participation in Jewish-Christian conversation, study and service to others. This focus is part of the larger movement within certain Christian communities that seeks to respect and value other expressions of religious insight such as Islam, Buddhism, Hinduism, and so forth.

All of the above places me within a certain "brand" of Christianity that seeks to be *inclusive* rather than *exclusive*. It attempts to take quite seriously the biblical claim that all human beings are made in the image of God and therefore worthy of respect.

It attempts to live the great mystery of the Trinity. It acknowledges Jesus, the human "face of God," who is at the same time the Word who is in communion with the Father and the Spirit, the Holy Trinity, one God, maker of heaven and earth and all that is and all that will be.

So it is within a historical context that I seek to follow Jesus as Christ. The ultimate value of all of the Christian traditions as I understand them is to provide a human context that supports members as they seek to know and to follow Christ and to continue his mission to embrace the coming of God's kingdom. These communities carry the traditions of prayer, study, liturgical worship and service to others that help members to recognize the presence of the risen Christ in themselves and in the world. Most Christians celebrate a special ceremony, variously known as the "breaking of the bread," "the Lord's Supper," "eucharist" (which means "thanksgiving") or "communion," which ritually recommits and sustains us in our religious lives. "In the Eucharistic meal, in the eating and drinking of the bread and wine, Christ grants communion with himself. God…acts, giving life to the Body of Christ and renewing each member" (World Council of Churches, *Baptism, Eucharist, and Ministry*, p. 10).

A common reality that identifies all of us as Christian is baptism, the sacrament that joins us to Christ and to one another as members of one body, the body of Christ. At each baptism and on particular days of the year, Episcopalians renew our baptismal covenant. It is a way of reminding ourselves of the basic framework of our lives. After affirming our belief in God, Father, Son and Spirit, we answer a series of questions:

+ Will you continue in the apostles' teaching and fellowship, in the breaking of the bread, and in the prayers?
   Response: I will, with God's help.

+ Will you persevere in resisting evil, and, whenever you fall into sin, repent and return to the Lord?
   Response: I will, with God's help.

+ Will you proclaim by word and example the Good News of God in Christ?
   Response: I will, with God's help.

+ Will you seek and serve Christ in all persons, loving your neighbor as yourself?
   Response: I will, with God's help.

◆ Will you strive for justice and peace among all people, and respect the dignity of every human being?

> *Response:* I will, with God's help.

There is also a prayer, familiar to all Christians, that expresses this same orientation to God. We call it the Lord's Prayer, given to us by Jesus. It reminds us of God's coming kingdom of justice and peace which Christians must help to establish:

> Our Father in heaven, hallowed be your Name,
> your kingdom come,
> your will be done on earth as in heaven.
> Forgive us our sins
> as we forgive those who sin against us.
> Save us from the time of trial,
> and deliver us from evil.
> For the kingdom, the power and the glory are yours,
> now and forever. Amen.

Reflection/Discussion Questions

1. What strikes you about the essay concerning the tradition of which you are not a member?
2. There are different movements in modern Judaism and there are different denominations of Christianity. Can you explain the main characteristics of the community to which you belong?
3. What do you think or feel that your identity as a Jew or a Christian requires of you?
4. The essay composed by the Jewish author made no direct reference to God. Is this simply the personal style of the writer or does it provide any insights into the differences or similarities between Christian and Jewish self-understanding?

Closing Prayer

Leader: God of all creation, your children have gathered here to discover the beauty of the diversity you have brought into being; a diversity that serves to give you glory. Help us to strive to be the peoples you have called us to be as we pray together in the words of the psalmist of long ago:

All: There is none like you among the gods, O Lord,
    and there are no deeds like yours.
All the nations you have made will come to bow before you, O
    Lord, and they will pay honor to your Name.
For you alone are great and perform wonders;
    you alone are God.
Teach us your way, O Lord; we will walk in your truth;
    let our hearts be undivided in reverence for your Name.
We will praise you, O Lord, our God, with all our hearts,
    and pay honor to your Name forever.
For your steadfast love toward us is great!
                    —*Based on Psalm 86:8–13a*

Leader: O God, we thank you for bringing us to this day. Grant that all of us will return safely to our homes. Gather us together again so that we can learn from each other of the greatness of your Name. And let us say:

All: Amen!

SESSION TWO

Celebrating the Principal Jewish Feasts

Claire G. Metzger and Ellen Zucker

The holidays have always been a special time for our families—a time to be together, take "time out" from our busy schedules and enjoy our warm and wonderful traditions. Like many people, our fondest holiday memories involve good food and family activities.

The Jewish year starts in autumn with ten days of reflection on the past and future, known as the Days of Awe, *Yamim Noraim.* The first two days, *Rosh Hashanah,* celebrate the New Year and the creation of the world. They usually occur in September, a hectic time for any family. A new school year has started, with parents and children adjusting to changing schedules, new wardrobes and different teachers. What a wonderful time to celebrate! At *Rosh Hashanah,* the *shofar* or ram's horn is sounded to acknowledge God's sovereignty. We enjoy the special treats of round *challah* (round bread to signify the circular passage of time), the apple dipped in honey, and honey cake for a sweet New Year. One of the highlights of *Rosh Hashanah* is the singing of *Avinu Malkeinu* (our Father, our King) and the other special melodies that are part of our High Holy Day liturgy. This holy season gives Jews the opportunity to pause and reflect on our deeds during the past year, mend fences and firmly resolve to try harder in the New Year.

Yom Kippur (the day of atonement) falls on the tenth day of the New Year. It is a day of fasting and recognition of communal failures: "we have sinned." The music of the day reminds us that we must strive to be better. In the days of the Temple in Jerusalem, the high priest would enter the Holy of Holies once a year on *Yom Kippur.* Today when we observe this day we read of that ancient service.

In biblical times, Jews were to make three pilgrimages to the Temple in Jerusalem each year on the harvest festivals of *Sukkot, Pesaḥ* and *Shavuot.* Today, *Sukkot* and *Pesaḥ* are mostly associated with celebrations in the home.

29

Only four days after the solemnity of *Yom Kippur,* we move quickly to *Sukkot.* This is a week-long fall harvest festival when we give thanks for the fall fruits and the goodness that surrounds us. Each family typically builds an outdoor *sukkah* or booth in which we dwell or eat meals as a reminder of our ancestors who were desert wanderers. We also recall the construction of temporary booths in the farmlands during the rich harvest season. In the *sukkah* we all sing the *kiddush,* recite special blessings and hear readings in which our ancestors are invited to join us in a special time of contentment.

Pesah or Passover is always especially memorable. After surviving a long, hard winter, this spring feast is very welcome. In many Jewish families, Passover is preceded by spring cleaning. The whole house, from basement to attic, is scrubbed; silver and brass are polished and curtains washed.

Pesah commemorates the exodus from Egypt. It is a holiday of freedom. The eight days of Passover begin with the Seder or Passover meal celebrated in the home on either the first or the first two evenings of the festival. There is a special menu consisting of foods that symbolize the exodus experience. *Matza,* unleavened bread, reminds us of the bread that couldn't be allowed to rise as the slaves rushed out of Egypt. *Haroset,* a pasty sweet substance, reminds us of the mortar used by our enslaved ancestors to make bricks, and *maror,* bitter herbs, recalls the sadness of our lives as slaves. Four cups of wine during the meal punctuate our prayers for freedom for all. The youngest child reads (or chants) four questions that prompt the reading of all or part of the *Haggadah,* the Passover story of the exodus from Egypt. This fulfills the obligation of the holiday to "teach your children" this pivotal story of Jewish history.

In ancient times, beginning on the second day of *Pesah* and continuing for seven weeks, a portion of barley, *omer,* was set aside as an offering for the poor. When the fifty-day period concluded, the third harvest festival, *Shavuot,* the Festival of Weeks was celebrated. Greek-speaking Jews later called the feast "Pentecost" because of this fifty-day interval. Originally marking the first fruits of the spring wheat harvest, it later became a celebration of the giving of the Torah to Moses on Mount Sinai. This is how the day is primarily observed today.

Only one holiday is mentioned in the Ten Commandments—the *Shabbat,* or Sabbath. Although *Shabbat* is not, per se, a festival, it is central to Judaism. The Bible says that in six days, God created the heavens and the earth, and on the seventh day God rested. Thus, we are commanded to make the seventh day holy by refraining from our normal pursuits and doing things differently—whether that be studying, resting or taking time out with our families. *Challah* (braided bread) is a traditional food eaten during *Shabbat.*

A beautiful ceremony we have at the end of *Shabbat* is *Havdalah,* meaning "separation" in Hebrew, and it is a ceremony in which we say goodbye to *Shabbat,* and prepare for the new week ahead. In that ceremony, we share some wine, smell sweet spices (usually cinnamon and nutmeg) and light a special multiwicked candle. These objects represent the special time we've had— a time we look forward to next week. It is also a time to sing songs and just have quiet time together—something all of us need.

Together, these feasts bring the Jewish history and tradition into our own world of today, enabling us to reaffirm and practice our religious identity and commitments.

Celebrating the Principal Christian Feasts

Paul R. Demers, S.C.

Every week Christians celebrate the memorial of Jesus' resurrection on Sunday, or what is called the Lord's Day, their primordial feast day. It recalls Jesus' victory over death and the life of God's kingdom which awaits us in the future.

What Sunday is to the week, Easter is to the whole year. At Easter the same central aspect of the Christian faith, the resurrection of Jesus, is commemorated in a richer manner. So even though Sunday is often called a little Easter, it might be more accurate to call Easter the great Sunday, since Sunday is the older feast.

In denominations with structured liturgical calendars, there are two major cycles of Christian feasts: Advent/Christmas and Lent/Easter/Pentecost. In this essay I will describe how these feasts are celebrated in the more liturgically centered Christian churches such as the Roman Catholic Church, the Orthodox Church and many Protestant and Reformed Communities.

"Dear friends, on this most holy night, when our Lord Jesus Christ passed from death to life, the Church invites her children throughout the world to come together in vigil and prayer. This is the Passover of the Lord." These solemn words begin the celebration of the Easter vigil.

Even though the precise relationship between the Christian *Pasch* and the Jewish *Pesah* (Passover) is riddled with questions, there is no doubt that Passover provided the context for the Last Supper of Jesus, his arrest, his trial, his passion and crucifixion. It was within the eight days of this Paschal festivity that his followers believed he rose from the dead on the first day of the week.

The earliest liturgical records situate the Paschal triduum, the central three-day celebration of the liturgical year, in the context of Passover, but the Paschal season is preceded by a forty-day period of preparation. It begins on

Ash Wednesday, the penitential day on which Christians, by signing themselves with ashes, remind themselves of their sinful moral situation. The day's liturgy invites conversion of heart that leads to greater fidelity to God through prayer, discipline and almsgiving as preparation for the Easter feasts.

The celebration of the triduum begins at sunset on Thursday, when the memorial of the Lord's Supper is recalled with a reading from Exodus 12, the description of the Passover meal. This is followed by a reading from Paul's first letter to the church at Corinth, which describes what Jesus did and said as he shared the bread and the cup at the Last Supper he had with his friends before his death. The thirteenth chapter of John's gospel is read, wherein the ritual washing of the feet is described. This ritual is reenacted after the reading. The celebration ends in silent vigil near the eucharist reserved for communion the following afternoon. The main Good Friday service is held midafternoon, if possible, since tradition has it that Jesus died at 3:00 P.M. After hearing the Suffering Servant song in Isaiah 53, the account of Jesus' passion and death is read. Then prayers of intercession for all the needs of the church and the world are voiced, a cross is venerated and the liturgy ends with a simple communion service consuming the bread consecrated the previous day.

Holy Saturday is a day of rest recalling the time of Jesus' resting in the tomb.

Easter begins with a vigil on Saturday night that includes a fire ritual and extended readings from the Old and New Testaments that conclude with the festive celebration of Jesus' resurrection. In the Roman Catholic tradition, these are followed by the rites of adult initiation into the church community: baptism, confirmation, eucharist. The Paschal triduum continues in the celebration of Easter on Sunday morning and ends with prayers on the evening of Easter Sunday.

The celebration continues for a "week of Sundays"—seven of them, each bearing the names *second, third, fourth,* and so forth, Sunday of Easter.

The Paschal season ends on the fiftieth day, the feast of Pentecost, which commemorates the outpouring of the Spirit of the Risen One on his followers. The readings of the day and the vigil relate to the Tower of Babel (Genesis 11), the giving of the Law on Sinai (Exodus 19), the valley of dry bones (Ezekiel 37), the outpouring of the Spirit (Joel 3), as well as the Christian account of the outpouring of the Spirit in the second chapter of the Acts of the Apostles, the Gospel of John, and Paul's first letter to the Corinthians (chapter 12).

The second great cycle of feasts centers around the birth of Jesus, celebrated on December 25 since the fourth century. Before then it had been celebrated on the Epiphany, January 6, wherein was commemorated not so much the birth but the "public manifestation" of Jesus to the magi, astrologers from the East (Matthew 2), his baptism by John at the Jordan River (Matthew 3:13–17) and his miraculous changing of water into wine at the wedding feast of Cana as recounted in John's gospel (2:1–11).

Eventually there was a movement to celebrate the nativity of Jesus. The Christmas cycle begins on December 25 and includes a midnight eucharist and lasts until the Sunday after January 6, when the baptism of Jesus is commemorated.

The period preceding the Christmas season is called Advent. It now begins on the fourth Sunday before Christmas. This season, while a period of preparation for the celebration of the first coming of Jesus, also invites reflection on his second coming at the end of time. This season is one of joyful and spiritual expectation, with readings that have messianic overtones, mainly from the Hebrew prophetic tradition. Included in the celebration of Advent are the harvest themes of grateful rejoicing and a focus on the end-times, when the world as we know it will give way to the Age to Come. Advent focuses on light at a time when days are getting shorter and darker. It is a time of hopeful expectation when light will overcome dark, when sin and evil will be overcome by grace and goodness, when fear, war and injustice will give way to love, peace and justice—all that the Messiah and the Messianic times invite us to wait for in hope.

The rest of the year, nearly half of it, is called "Ordinary Time." It is a time when the weeks are numerically ordered from one to thirty-four to keep track of the assigned readings and prayers.

Christian feasts, like all holy days and holidays, find their power in the roots of ritual, a tradition-bound patterned behavior, that transcends the present moment and is connected with age-old history. The particular customs of celebration, of course, also vary greatly among the many ethnic groups and cultures that compose Christianity. The celebration of ancient yet ever new feasts defines our very identity and provides patterns of prayer and worship that are both the source and summit of the liturgy of life—the ongoing love of God and neighbor manifested in a life of peace and justice lived not only in our places of worship but in our homes and places of work and recreation.

Reflection/Discussion Questions

1. What holiday or feast in your tradition was most meaningful to you as a child? Which is most meaningful to you now as an adult?
2. What holiday or feast of the other religious tradition most appeals to you or would you most want to know more about?
3. The Sabbath, because it occurs weekly, is often overlooked. What could you do, as either a Christian or a Jew, to make your Sabbath observances more significant to you and your family?
4. How does the commercialization of religious feasts affect you? How do you think it affects the members of the other religious tradition?

Closing Prayer

At the beginning of the prayer, the lights should be dimmed. A large candle is prominently displayed.

Leader: We begin our prayer together by hearing the words that begin the Bible:

Reader: When God began to create heaven and earth—the earth being unformed and void, with darkness over the surface of the deep and a wind from God sweeping over the water—God said, "Let there be light"; and there was light. God saw that the light was good, and God separated the light from the darkness (Genesis 1:1–4).

Leader: As our candle is lighted, let us pray together this meditation:

All: May the brightness of this candle banish all gloom, anxiety and care from our hearts and from the hearts of our loved ones. May our sharing of shalom together bring us peace and serenity, joy and rest. Keep aglow within us, O God, a spirit of gratitude for your many blessings, so that we may know the sweet taste of contentment and the rich harvest of sharing. Kindle in our world a deeper love for one another, for our people and for all your children. And let us say, "Amen!"

Leader: Let us hear from the Christian Scriptures a lesson about light taught by one Son of Israel's Covenant, Jesus of Nazareth:

Reader: "You are the light of the world. A city built on a hill cannot be hid. No one after lighting a lamp puts it under a bushel basket, but on a lampstand, and it gives light to all in the house. In the same way, let your light shine before others, so that they may see your good works and give glory to your Father in heaven" (Matthew 5:14–16).

Leader: We have begun to experience the light of understanding together. Let us go forth from here, knowing that we should share this light with others. And let us say:

All: Amen!

SESSION THREE

Jewish Sabbath Worship

Arthur F. Starr

While *Shabbat* (Sabbath) services will vary among the major movements within Judaism, they will also vary from one congregation to another within the same movement. Yet most services will contain certain common rubrics and prayers.

The *Shabbat* morning service begins with "warm-ups"—that is, readings, psalms and hymns that prepare the worshiper for prayer or set a mood. These might include the *Birkat HaShachar* (morning blessings) and *Pesuke DeZimra* (selections of psalms).

The first major element of the service is the *Sh'ma* and its blessings. It is preceded by the call to worship, "Praise the One to whom our praise is due," followed by the congregation's response, "Praised be the One to whom our praise is due now and forever." The *Sh'ma* is a statement of the unity of God, professed by traditional Jews three times a day at prayer, before going to sleep and as the very last words of life: "Hear, O Israel, the Eternal One is our God, the Eternal God alone." This is followed by two prayers of praise to God for creating the orderly cycles of nature and thanking God for the abundant love for the people Israel, shown by the giving of the Torah.

After the *Sh'ma* the verses following it in Deuteronomy chapter 6 are read. These tell of our obligation to love God, "with all of our heart, soul and might." Paragraphs speaking of redemption follow, leading up to the Song of the Red Sea, from Exodus, chapter 15:11, "Who is like You, Eternal One, among the mighty?…"

The central part of the *Shabbat* worship service is a section of prayers known as the *Amidah* (standing) or *T'filah* (prayer). It consists of seven separate parts. The first three and the last three are part of the weekday service as well, but on *Shabbat* a special section about the Sabbath replaces the thirteen intermediary prayers of the weekday. These are omitted on *Shabbat* because they deal with sorrow, repentance, sin, suffering and other human problems that might detract from the enjoyment of the Sabbath. The seven sections of the *Shabbat Amidah* are:

1. *Avot*—tells of the merits of our ancestors Abraham, Isaac and Jacob (and increasingly of Sarah, Rebekkah, Leah and Rachel) in the hope (expectation?) that God will be gracious to us because of their merit.
2. *Gevurot*—recalls God's power in all of nature, in renewing our lives and in providing immortality (everlasting life?).
3. *Kedusha*—the Sanctification, is a praise of God that includes the vision of Isaiah 6:3 and the words, "Holy, Holy, Holy, is the Eternal God…."
4. *Kedushat Hayom*—the Sanctification of the Day, is inserted in place of the intermediary benedictions of the weekday service. This section speaks of the holiness of the Sabbath day and our obligations to keep and rejoice in it.
5. *Avodah*—a section that asks that our worship (service) be acceptable to God, referring back to the sacrificial offering by the priests when the Temple in Jerusalem was standing.
6. *Hodaah*—a thanksgiving to God in general terms for all of our blessings.
7. *Birkat Shalom*—is the prayer for peace. It concludes the *Amidah* and is often followed by a period of silent meditation.

The Torah reading is the highlight of a Sabbath morning worship service. A dramatic moment occurs when the Torah is taken from the Ark in which it abides and is processed through the congregation. Individual members of the congregation are honored as they are called to the Torah to recite the blessings that precede and follow the Torah reading itself. These blessings thank God for the gift of the Torah. A portion of the weekly Torah selection is read. Over the course of the Jewish year, the entire Torah will be read in sections *(parashiyot)*.

An additional reading from the Prophets usually follows the Torah reading, a selection that is somehow related in its content or subject to the weekly Torah portion.

Following the return of the Torah to the Ark, a *D'rash* (interpretation) or a *D'var Torah* (a word of Torah) or a sermon might take place.

The *Shabbat* morning service nears its conclusion with the *Alenu* prayer. This speaks of our unique destiny and obligations as a people and expresses the hope that one day all the world shall worship one God.

Following *Alenu* is a mourner's prayer, the *Kaddish*, which is a praise of God. It is recited when deceased loved ones are remembered on or near the anniversary of their death. In many congregations, the entire congregation recites the prayer, not just mourners.

The service concludes with the singing of one or more hymns and, in some congregations, a closing benediction.

Christian Sunday Worship

Barbara Anne Radtke

Each weekend, Christian congregations gather to worship in marvelously diverse ways, making it almost impossible to predict exactly what a visitor might encounter in any one specific Christian worship service. For all this variety, however, a guest in almost any Christian congregation might expect that the worship would include a welcome, a proclamation or reading of various biblical texts, preaching, prayer and possibly music. Depending upon the denominational/church affiliation, a communion service may always be included or it may be a rare or occasional option.

Roman Catholics gather each Saturday evening or Sunday for worship in a service that is known as the *mass*. It consists of two major parts: the liturgy of the Word and the liturgy of the eucharist. The liturgy of the Word includes three readings: one from the Hebrew Scriptures, one from the Epistles or Letters in the New Testament, and one from a gospel. A priest or deacon preaches a homily or a reflection on the readings.

All masses include a liturgy of the eucharist. In this part of the mass, the priest consecrates bread and wine, praying one of the four various eucharistic prayers that he can select, and then distributes this sacrament to the faithful who choose to go to communion and receive the consecrated bread and wine. Although it is understood differently in the various Christian denominations, Christians believe that Jesus Christ is with them when they share the consecrated bread and drink the cup. Following communion, there is a short concluding rite. Almost always, a Sunday Mass has some music. There are various hymns that may be sung as processionals, as accompaniments to communion and as recessionals. Certain parts of the mass may be sung too. There can be a wide variety of musical accompaniment that can range from organ to guitar.

Virtually all Christian churches proclaim some reading from Scripture at each worship service. A presiding minister offers a sermon or homily. The texts chosen may be selected in advance because they are indicated by a lectionary, a book that outlines a cycle of readings throughout a year or a group of years. A number of Christian churches and denominations share a common lectionary that outlines Sunday readings on a three-year cycle. If a congregation does not follow a lectionary, the texts are selected by the presiding minister. Technically, a homily is a reflection on the Scripture that has been read and a sermon is a moral or theological exhortation that may not be tied to the text.

The Word correctly preached was a hallmark of the Protestant Reformation in Europe during the sixteenth century. Therefore, Protestant churches historically have put greater emphasis on preaching than Catholic or Orthodox Christians and generally, even today, give more time in their services for the sermon or homily. This time may be extended if there is no plan for a communion service on a given Sunday.

Orthodox Christians, some Episcopalians and some Protestants such as Lutherans worship every Sunday with a service that includes communion. The decision about the frequency of communion services in any congregation depends upon the history of the practice of both the local congregation and the church/denomination to which the congregation is affiliated. The liturgy for Orthodox Christians and the mass for Catholics always includes communion or, as both traditions would say, the eucharist. Some Protestant churches feel that too frequent communion detracts from hearing and preaching the Word of God.

The manner in which communion is received can vary greatly from one congregation or denomination to another. I have a very delightful memory of one class that I taught in which students from the Greek Orthodox Church, the Roman Catholic Church and the United Church of Christ spontaneously shared the ways they received communion. The Greek Orthodox student received the blessed bread that had been dipped in the blessed wine from a small spoon. The Roman Catholic came forward from a pew to form a line with other parishioners. One at a time, the Catholics received a flat (unleavened), wheat wafer and were separately offered a sip of wine. The congregant from the United Church of Christ received a small cube of leavened bread and an individual small cup of grape juice. This was passed to her in her pew in a specially designed tray that held dozens of little cups or glasses. Congregants helped themselves but waited until all had been served before ingesting the bread and juice. The back of each pew had little holders to hold the empty cups. The delight for me in this impromptu sharing among these students was that each story was greeted as a novelty because each student was unaware of all the various ways of distributing communion among Christian congregations!

The order of a service may vary greatly. Episcopalian congregations follow one of the choices of the orders of service and styles of prayer found in the *Book of Common Prayer.* Protestant churches may follow denominational guidelines or may be fully dependent on an order of service devised by their pastors. Catholics follow an order of service designated by an official book called a sacramentary. Orthodox churches follow the rubrics and orders prescribed by their particular churches.

Music will also vary greatly, even within one congregation or within the same family of traditions. A strong example of such variety is a folk mass at one hour in a Catholic church and a choir mass with Gregorian chant at the next. One Baptist church may be known for its gospel choir and another for its congregational singing. Historically, a church may trace its roots back to the Reformation, where congregations were restricted from using any music except those based on scriptural texts. Another church may come from a tradition such as Methodism, in which hymns and congregational singing are very close to the identity of being a Christian. For most Orthodox Christians, the use of chant, often by a choir, is integral to the celebration of the liturgy. The richness of the Christian tradition, not only in its denominational/church diversity but also in its ethnic and cultural variety, can often be best experienced through its wide range of worship music.

The very entry into a worship space may characterize the community and its traditions. Indications will be everywhere: stained glass windows or clear ones; pews in a row, pews in a circular fashion or no pews at all; icons or statues or bare church walls; the smells of candle wax or incense or freshly cut flowers; the altar as central, the pulpit as the main feature or the sanctuary closed off by a "holy" screen. Each of these features is an outgrowth of a theological or pastoral decision made sometime in history that now influences the way these Christians worship.

In each worship experience, there usually are a number of persons involved. Usually a guest will first encounter a greeter or an usher who will help the person to locate a seat and obtain a prayer book or program containing the order of service. (In some Orthodox churches, congregants may stand in a large open space, so there will be no pews.) There is a presiding priest or minister. This person may be accompanied by others who also go to the sanctuary area during the service. There may also be various people who read the scripture or who help distribute communion. There may be musicians both for accompaniment and/or a choir for song. There may be numerous people who are working behind the scenes—to prepare the communion, to take care of the cups, plates, linens or other items used during the service, or to prepare the bulletin listing the order of service. When the service is over, it may be common for the presiding priest/minister to say farewell to each person as she or he leaves the church. Or there may be an invitation to join other members of the congregation in a hall or church basement for coffee and for fellowship.

Reflection/Discussion Questions

1. In order to summarize the wide variations of practice within the different Jewish movements and Christian denominations, this session's essays had to be somewhat general. Based on your experiences within your own religious community, are there further descriptions or details you would like to offer your dialogue partners?
2. What similarities do you see between Jewish and Christian weekly worship?
3. What differences in practice or emphasis do you see between Jewish and Christian weekly worship or among the various expressions of your own faith tradition?
4. Are there elements in the other community's weekly celebrations that you admire or would like to see become part of your own religion's practices?

Closing Prayer

In a prominent place, a table might be placed. On it could be a candle, a Torah scroll or Tanakh *and a Christian Bible. Light the candle as the prayer begins.*

Leader: Both Jews and Christians possess ancient scriptural books that they consider holy and inspired. Some of these scriptures are shared by both religions, although they have been interpreted differently over the ages. When they gather for weekly prayer, both Jews and Christians turn to the scriptures for guidance and inspiration today. Now, therefore, let us praise God for the gift of sacred writings with the word of a psalm from long ago:

All: *(May be proclaimed in alternating groups.)*

1.	2.

Happy are those whose way is blameless,
    who follow the teaching of the Lord.
Happy are those who observe Your decrees,
    who turn to God wholeheartedly.
	The Lord is my portion,
	    I have resolved to keep Your words.
	Your word is a lamp to my feet,
	    a light for my path.

Your decrees are wondrous;
    rightly do I observe them.
The words You inscribed give light,
    and grant understanding to the simple.

I open my mouth wide, I pant,
    longing for your commandments.
Turn to me and be gracious to me,
    as is Your rule with those who
    love Your name.

All: Open our eyes, that we may perceive the wonder of Your teaching.

Leader: Let us go in peace and ponder the mystery of our kinship in God.

All: Amen.

Adapted from Psalm 119.

SESSION FOUR

Jewish Understandings of Messiah

Arthur F. Starr

The English word *messiah* is derived from the Hebrew word *mashiah*. In its broadest sense, it refers to a person who has been anointed for a certain mission on behalf of God or God's people. In the Hebrew Scriptures, priests are characterized as God's anointed, and once even a pagan emperor is so described (*see* Isaiah 45:1), but the term is most often used of King David or his dynastic heirs.

This "royal messianism" first appears in 2 Samuel 7, in which God is pictured as promising David that he and his heirs will sit forever on a victorious throne. Similarly, the "royal psalms," including Psalms 2, 72 and 110, were probably sung at important royal events such as coronations. They celebrated the close relationship between the king and God with such metaphors as divine sonship (2:7) and the divine begetting of the king (110:3). As messiah, or God's anointed, the Davidic king was hailed as God's son, who was victorious in battle, administered God's justice, saved God's people from external threats and was personally righteous. The king was also seen to epitomize the whole People. If the king was virtuous, so were the People, and vice-versa.

As time passed, it became clear that not all of David's successors on the throne were worthy of such accolades. The reigns of evil or self-serving kings prompted a longing for a true king who would rule according to God's wishes. The eighth-century B.C.E. prophet, Isaiah of Jerusalem, is particularly notable for speaking about a divine restoration of the monarchy to righteousness. In Isaiah 7:14–17 and 9:1–7, he anticipates that a righteous king is about to be born in the court of the wicked King Ahaz, thereby proving that God is indeed with the people in the person of a just king. Isaiah probably felt that his hope was fulfilled by the subsequent reign of King Hezekiah, remembered as one of Judah's greatest kings. The prophet Micah (5:1–6) expressed a similar wish

51

for a Davidic king to emerge from Bethlehem to protect the people and reunite the divided tribes of Israel.

Such short-term yearnings for the birth of a Godly king from David's heirs became unthinkable once the Davidic monarchy itself came to an end after the Babylonian conquest of Judah. When the Babylonian exile ended and a Second Temple was built, the people were ruled by the priesthood.

In this Second Temple period (538 B.C.E. to 70 C.E., including the ministry of Jesus), expectations about a coming messiah could not be grounded in the birth of the next Davidic heir. They were dependent on an intervention of God to anoint human or heavenly agent or agents who would restore Israel to independent greatness and bring justice and peace. In the biblical book of Daniel, written in the second century B.C.E., there is a visionary description of "one like a son of man coming with the clouds of heaven. And he came to the Ancient One and was presented before him. To him was given dominion and glory and kingship, that all people, nations, and languages should serve him" (7:13–14a). Probably originally a corporate reference to all the Jewish people, this son of man figure coming on the clouds later took on messianic associations and was very influential in early Christianity. A similar concept is found in a roughly contemporary section of the nonbiblical *First Book of Enoch*. A heavenly individual, variously called "the Anointed One," "the Righteous One," "the son of man," and, most often, "the Chosen One," is selected by God to be the judge of all humanity who will vindicate the righteous. This celestial champion is described as secretly dwelling with God from the creation, but who is now about to defeat the enemies of the righteous.

And so, by the first century B.C.E. and the first century C.E., some Jews didn't think in terms of a coming messiah at all. Some anticipated a Moses-like figure who would provide perfect instruction in the Torah and so establish God's will in the world. Some hoped for the restoration of the Davidic monarchy. Other Jews, notably the Dead Sea Scroll people at Qumran, wrote of several messianic scenarios which highlighted a priestly messiah who would purify the Temple and offer perfect sacrifices there.

The main point in all this is that in Second Temple Judaism there was no uniform set of expectations about a coming messiah or messiahs. Whether conceived of as human or angelic, as Mosaic, Davidic or priestly, those Jews who thought in messianic terms read the older priestly and royal messianic scriptural passages in ways that substantiated their own expectations for the future.

The birth of Christianity in the first century C.E. had little impact on Judaism for centuries. Once Christianity became a significant political force, especially when it became the preferred religion in the Roman Empire in the fourth century C.E., then the rabbis had to respond to the Church's messianic claims. After the loss of the Temple in 70 C.E., the earlier diversity of Jewish messianic expectations had already begun to become more streamlined. By the fourth century the rabbis formalized the process.

Contrary to the beliefs of the Christians, the rabbis stressed the concept of an earthly Messiah—a human being descended from King David. This became the prevailing concept in rabbinic Judaism, as is evidenced by the Prayer for the Coming of the Messiah, in which the Messiah is called the "descendant of David" or the "Branch of David." The Jewish understanding of the mission of the Messiah was also formalized at this time: he would liberate Israel from pagan authorities and set up his own kingdom of peace. Such a notion probably grounded the acclamation of Simon bar Kokhba, the leader of the second Jewish revolt against Rome in 132–35 C.E., as the Messiah by the famous Rabbi Akiba.

No doubt eventually written as a polemical answer to Christian teaching, another messianic figure appears in the Midrash (rabbinic homiletic collections) known as the Messiah, son of Joseph. He is first mentioned in the talmudic *Tractate Sukkah,* where the statements about him speak of his fate, namely, to fall in battle. Details about him are found in later literature of the Midrash, where he will precede the Messiah son of David and will gather the children of Israel around him, march to Jerusalem and eventually be killed, buried in Jerusalem and hidden by the angels until Messiah son of David comes. It must be emphasized, however, that "messiah" was not a dominant topic in the rabbinic writings.

Since that time, the messianic concept has been a hope to Jews in times of stress and persecution. Even in the depths of despair, most recently as they were marched into the gas chambers of the Nazi genocide, Jews recited the words, "*Ani Ma-amin*—I believe with perfect faith in the coming of the Messiah, and though he tarry still I believe."

Among traditional Jews of today, particularly the more Orthodox, there remains the belief in the coming of a Messiah, a descendant of David, who will enter Jerusalem through the Messiah's Gate and defeat the forces of evil, bringing about God's kingdom on earth. The Messiah might come at any time, particularly in times of great distress for Jews. This expectation is ritually symbolized, for example, at the circumcision ceremony of a Jewish child, at which a chair is usually set aside for Elijah. Since Elijah is the expected forerunner of the Messiah, it is anticipated that Elijah would come and occupy the seat reserved for him should the child being circumcised actually be the Messiah. The messianic hopes of the Passover Seder likewise include a cup of wine for Elijah.

Beginning in the nineteenth century, the liberal movements in Judaism replaced the concept of an individual Messiah with the idea of a Messianic Age, a time when God's kingdom will be a reality. These movements emphasize the responsibility of all humanity to help bring it about. Thus, while more traditional Jews await the coming of the Messiah, more liberal Jews work for the coming of the Messianic Age. Both agree, in contradistinction to Christianity, that neither the Messiah nor the Messianic Age has yet come.

A joke about this difference between Jews and Christians has circulated recently: The Messiah finally arrives and enters Jerusalem through the Messiah's Gate. He/She is greeted by throngs of people milling around the Old City. Television and radio coverage is extensive and all the world is listening or watching this dramatic scene. One reporter puts a microphone in front of the Messiah's mouth, hoping to get the biggest news story of all: "Tell me," says the reporter, "is this your first visit to Jerusalem?" A long silence occurs. The reporter speaks up, repeating again, "Is this your first visit to Jerusalem?" There is another long silence. Finally, the Messiah leans toward the reporter and speaks clearly into the microphone: "No comment!"

Christian Understandings of Messiah

Philip A. Cunningham

As mentioned in the previous essay, in the time of Jesus there was no general or universal set of expectations about a coming messiah. In that Second Temple Period, some Jews didn't think a messiah was coming and others thought several different sorts of messianic figures would one day appear. There is no evidence that any Jews were anticipating that a messiah would suffer. The only common element among the vast diversity of messianic expectations in Jesus' time was that somehow the Age to Come of God's justice and peace, in which Israel would be restored, would be established at last.

The life of Jesus, though, produced new ways of thinking about a messiah among some Jews. His followers who witnessed his execution as "King of the Jews" later experienced him as still living in transcendent glory. They judged that the Crucified One had been vindicated by God. They concluded that the kingdom of God that Jesus had constantly proclaimed must indeed be breaking into human history and that his resurrection was a spectacular manifestation of its dawning. Although Jesus himself may have avoided the term "messiah" during his ministry, possibly because of its vagaries of meaning, to his followers who sensed his resurrection it was clear that Jesus must be a messiah-king who was establishing the Age to Come.

Armed with this conviction, the Jewish believers in the messianic status of the Crucified and Raised One began to reread the Hebrew Scriptures for greater understanding. Their method of interpreting the biblical texts was identical to that of their Jewish contemporaries, but their particular perspective was a Jesus-centered one.

They saw the divine sonship language of the royal messianic psalms as uniquely applicable to, and maybe even predictive of, Jesus. They understood the suffering servant songs of Isaiah of the Exile as especially pertinent to

Jesus' death; and so those songs, which had not been viewed as messianic before, were now woven into the image of the Crucified One's messiahship. Priestly images of a messiah were absorbed into their reflections on Jesus' self-sacrifice on the cross. In short, they adapted and combined helpful earlier messianic ideas in order to clarify for themselves the significance of Jesus.

Indeed, as their creative work unfolded, it soon became clear to early Christians that "messiah" was an inadequate term to capture fully Jesus' importance for them. Its use as a title dwindled fairly quickly, becoming in its Greek form a sort of surname instead. He was known as Jesus Christ. Because these first members of the church felt Jesus' continuing presence most strongly when they assembled to memorialize him at fellowship meals, over time they began to pray to him at such gatherings. Therefore, the titles which replaced "messiah" in importance were the far more transcendent ones of "Lord" and "Son of God." They expressed the divine status of the Crucified-and-Raised One to whom they prayed.

Jesus referred to as "Christ," therefore, expressed new dimensions of thinking about Israel's "messiah." Unlike previous messianic scenarios in which the messiah(s) was expected to usher in God's reign in its fullness, Jesus Christ was seen as the one who inaugurated the reign in an embryonic way. Like yeast in dough, Jesus had begun the inevitable transformation of the world. When the Lord Christ returned in glory on the clouds of heaven (the "son of man" image in Daniel 9), he would establish God's justice and universal shalom. Finally, for these earliest believers in Jesus' resurrection, "messiah" became linked with divinity, an association not prevalent in prior Jewish traditions. Indeed, this linkage was so stressed that messiah soon functioned in the church as a name more than as a descriptive title.

At various times over the centuries, some Christians would become excited about the prospect that Jesus Christ's return, or *parousia,* was about to happen. Some of them imagined that the world was soon coming to a cataclysmic end, whereupon Christ would reestablish order and vindicate the righteous. This happened in the Middle Ages, for example, as the Christian calendar turned to the year 1000, and some Christians will no doubt become similarly agitated as the year 2000 approaches. In the minds of most Christians, however, the Second Coming of Jesus has been postponed into the unforeseeable future.

Putting aside such apocalyptic ideas, it is not uncommon today to hear someone say, "Christians believe that the Messiah has already come, while Jews are still waiting." Like many such simple statements of complex realities, this remark contains some truth, but it obscures much truth as well. Its main difficulty is that modern Jews and Christians do not mean the same thing by the word "messiah." Jews today who use the expression believe that with the

Messiah's advent the Age to Come will prevail. Clearly that New Age has not yet dawned. The lion does not lie down with the lamb, the swords have not been beaten into plowshares, nor are peace and justice universal. Observing reality with this understanding, Jews cannot accept the Christian assertion that the Messiah has come.

Indeed, if Christians defined "messiah" in this ultimate sense, they would have to relegate the Messiah's work to the future. One of the earliest New Testament assertions of Jesus' messianic identity does precisely this: "Turn to God so that your sins may be wiped out, so that times of refreshing may come from the presence of the Lord, and that he might send the Messiah appointed for you, that is, Jesus, who must remain in heaven until the time of universal restoration that God announced long ago through his holy prophets" (Acts 3:19–21). While this very early understanding was quickly supplanted by others, it describes the resurrected Jesus as a messiah-designate who will undertake his messianic mission in the (near) future.

Naturally, as time passed, Christians revised the meaning of "messiah." In interfaith settings, it might help clarify things to refer to the Christian perspective by speaking about Jesus as the Christ, rather than as the Messiah. Unlike Jews who see the Messiah's coming as simultaneous with the fullness of the Age to Come, Christians see Jesus Christ as the one who has irreversibly inaugurated God's kingdom. They believe that Christ Jesus has initiated God's kingdom in a nascent form, like a tiny mustard seed that will grow to mammoth proportions. Recognizing its present incompleteness, Christians still pray that God's kingdom will come, and they hold that when Christ returns in glory the Age to Come will be definitively realized.

Although Jews and Christians do not now mean the same thing by "messiah," there is this important commonality: both communities feel obligated to set the stage for the arrival of the Anointed One, however that figure is perceived. A 1985 Vatican instruction expressed the idea this way:

> Furthermore, in underlining the [unfinished] dimension of Christianity we shall reach a greater awareness that the people of God of the Old and New Testaments are tending toward a like end in the future: the coming or the return of the Messiah—even if they start from two different points of view. It is more clearly understood that the person of the Messiah is not only a point of division for the people of God but also a point of convergence.... Attentive to the same God who has spoken, hanging on the same word, we have to witness to one same memory and one common hope in [the One] who is the master of history. We must also accept our responsibility to prepare the world for the coming of the Messiah by working together for social justice, respect for the rights of persons and nations and for social and international reconciliation. To this we are driven, Jews and Christians,

by the command to love our neighbor, by a common hope for the kingdom of God, and by the great heritage of the Prophets. Transmitted soon enough by catechesis, such a conception would teach young Christians in a practical way to cooperate with Jews, going beyond simple dialogue.

(Vatican Commission for Religious Relations with the Jews, "Notes on the Correct Way to Present Jews and Judaism in Preaching and Catechesis in the Roman Catholic Church," II, 10–11.)

Surely, our collaborative work as Jews and Christians will be advanced by more clearly understanding each other's traditions. Our different yet complementary views of "messiah" are concepts that can be used to bring us together rather than divide us. As related Peoples of God, we can become allies rather than rivals, and thus be more effective in bringing God to the world.

Reflection/Discussion Questions

1. Give examples of how the word *messiah* has been used in different ways by different people over time.
2. Explain to your dialogue partners how you understood their tradition's views about the Messiah and if your understanding was modified in any way by this week's essay.
3. Why is it important to understand that Jesus' Jewish contemporaries did not have uniform expectations about a coming messiah?
4. What are the most important things that should be taught to both Jews and Christians about the subject of messiah?

Closing Prayer

Leader: Jews and Christians have a common longing and mission on behalf of the Age to Come. Let us listen to how some Hebrew writers envisioned this glorious time when God's will shall prevail over all of creation:

Reader 1:
Faithfulness and truth meet; justice and well-being kiss. Truth springs up from the earth; justice looks down from heaven. The Lord also shows his bounty; our land yields its produce. Justice goes before God as He sets out on His way (Psalm 85:11–14).

Reader 2:
Then the eyes of the blind shall be opened, and the ears of the deaf shall be unstopped. Then the lame shall leap like a deer. And the tongue of the dumb shall shout aloud. (Isaiah 35: 5–6).

Reader 3:
For instruction shall come forth from Zion; the word of the Lord from Jerusalem. Then God will judge among the many peoples; and arbitrate for the multitude of nations, however distant. And they shall beat their swords into plowshares, and their spears into pruning hooks. Nation shall not take up sword against nation; they shall never again know war (Micah 4:3).

Reader 4:

Then the wolf shall dwell with the lamb; the leopard lie down with the kid; the calf, the beast of prey, and the fatling together, with a little child to herd them. The cow and the bear shall graze; their young shall lie down together. And the lion, like the ox, shall eat straw. A babe shall play over a viper's hole, and an infant pass his hand over an adder's den. In all of My sacred mount nothing evil or vile shall be done; for the land shall be filled with devotion to the Lord as water covers the sea (Isaiah 11:6–9).

Leader: On each of our respective Sabbaths, Jews and Christians both look forward to that day, that Messianic Age, when, in the words of Paul of Tarsus, "God will mean everything to everyone" (1 Corinthians 15:28). Let us conclude our time together today by recommitting ourselves to the Age to Come by singing this song:

Bashanah Habaah

Ba-sha-na ha-ba-ah, ney-shev al ha-mir-pes-et
ve-nis-por tzip-o-rim no-de-dot.
Yel-a-dim be-chuf-sha ye-sa-ch-ku to-fes-et
beyn ha-ba-yit le-veyn ha-so-dot.

Chorus
Ode ti-reh, ode ti-reh ka-ma-tov yi-h'-yeh, ba-sha-na, ba-sha-na ha-ba-ah!
Ode ti-reh, ode ti-reh ka-ma-tov yi-h'-yeh, ba-sha-na, ba-sha-na ha-ba-ah!

In the Year that will come, we'll live in peace together, without war, without care, without fear.
And the children will play, without wond'ring whether in the sky dark new clouds will appear.

Chorus
Wait and see, wait and see, what a world this will be,
    if we care, if we share, you and me!
Wait and see, wait and see, what a world this will be,
    if we care, if we share, you and me!
Repeat Hebrew chorus

SESSION FIVE

A Jew Looks at the
Two-Thousand Year Encounter

Joel Klein

In the dark days of 1938 when Nazi atrocities threatened European Jewry and the whole civilized world, Pope Pius XI was reading from a prayer book which he had received from Belgian pilgrims. One prayer asked God to accept the prayers of Catholics with the same favor with which God had viewed Abraham's willingness to sacrifice his beloved son, Isaac. Inspired by the passage, the Pope declared, "We call Abraham, our father, our ancestor. Anti-Semitism is incompatible with the sublime thought and reality in the text.... Through Christ and in Christ, we are of the spiritual lineage of Abraham. Spiritually we are Semites."

While the acknowledgment of a shared spiritual heritage forms a common ground for both Jews and Christians, over the centuries both sides, for historical, social and religious reasons, tried to distance themselves from each other.

After the miracle that Christians had survived the first three hundred years of their history, they finally achieved political power by becoming the "state religion" of the Roman Empire through the declaration of Emperor Theodosius I in 380 C.E. After successfully creating an international church and a uniform New Testament and armed with the might of the Empire, the church engaged in a serious effort to unify all people in one faith, to root out heretics, and to curb competing faiths.

From the second through fourth centuries, Christianity's main rival was Judaism. Once Christians gained access to imperial political power, they tried to curb Jewish influence and prestige. Laws were passed with discriminatory provisions against Jews. For example, the Laws of Constantine II, enacted in 399, banned intermarriage between Jewish men and Christian women; the

Laws of Theodosius II in 439 prohibited Jews to hold high positions in government; and the Laws of Justinian, passed in 531, barred Jews from appearing in court as witnesses against Christians.

Although at first sight these regulations may seem derogatory against the Jews, it is important to notice that they were directed against all heretics and pagans and served two purposes: protecting the infant religion from the competition of other religions and assuring that key posts in government would be occupied by coreligionists. It should be observed that the Jews of the time were not immediately or significantly disturbed by these new ordinances. In fact, the marriage laws were welcomed since the Jewish communities imposed similar laws against intermarriage upon themselves, based on the Book of Deuteronomy.

However, the lives of many Jews became far more precarious in the Middle Ages. For centuries, there had been Jewish communities throughout the entire Roman Empire. When, by the end of the sixth century, a series of invasions had contributed to the downfall of the western Roman Empire, Jews shared a common misery with other Europeans. The church dispatched monks to the Germanic newcomers to baptize them and save their souls. By 1000, "Christendom" covered the map of Europe, and only Finland and Lithuania were left to be Christianized.

Still, Christian dominance of medieval Europe was incomplete: unconverted Jews, unlike the resisting pagans and other nonbelievers, had not been killed. Because the civilization of the Middle Ages was religiously oriented, it was paramount that the Jews be converted. Therefore, in the hope that their conversion would be achieved, the policy became to protect the Jews, yet to keep them on the lowest viable economic level to assure their survival. Applying this principle, Christendom took a lenient attitude toward the obstinate Jews, being content with their marginal place in medieval life.

After the eleventh century, new and serious Christian customs and habits diminished medieval Jewish life. Such practices included requiring Jews to wear different forms of humiliating garb, promulgating charges that Jews ritually murdered Christian children or desecrated sacred hosts, confining Jews in ghettoes and periodic massacres of Jewish communities.

To illustrate the last item, soldiers of the First Crusade sought to remove "the infidels at home" by massacring over forty Jewish communities in central Europe. In these attacks, Jews were stoutly, though ineffectively, defended by most bishops. From January to June 1096, it is estimated that up to ten thousand Jews died, probably one-third to one-fourth of the Jewish people of Germany and northern France.

In the Protestant Reformation of the sixteenth century, Jews were the targets of Reformers and Roman Catholics alike. For instance, Martin Luther stated, "If I had been a Jew and seen such blockheads and locusts ruling and teaching Christianity, I would have become a swine rather than a Christian, because they have treated Jews like dogs and not like human beings." He hoped that the Jews would convert to the new form of Christianity he had helped develop. When they did not, he vociferously denounced Jews as vigorously as had the pre-Reformation church, stating, if "the Jews refuse to be converted, we ought not suffer them or bear with them any longer." Thereafter, with but few exceptions, animosity and discrimination against the Jews continued as the general policy in both Protestant and Catholic Europe.

With the coming of the eighteenth century, new emerging liberal political voices sounded a novel idea that religious differences were not justifications for civil restrictions and that if the Jews were equally afforded economic, professional and educational freedom, all society would benefit. But only a bloody and sordid upheaval such as the French Revolution could overthrow the alliance of clergy, the economically powerful and the politically conservative, who intended to maintain aristocratic privileges and to keep the Jews in their place. This Revolution was, "to abolish Christianity and establish a regime of Reason," leading the Jews to believe that the secular liberals who favored the removal of the church from its position of influence within the State would also support movements to emancipate them from their marginal status. Churches and clergy in general sought to maintain the centuries-old status quo in Christian Europe and to deny Jews the fruit of freedom.

After Waterloo in 1815, Pope Pius VII restricted the Jews to the ghetto and condoned coercive missionary activities. Spain renewed the Inquisition. Germany, under the influence of Goethe, reimposed medieval conditions on the Jews; they were expelled from Lubeck, Bremen and the faculty of the University of Berlin. From 1870 until World War I and even afterward in Germany, anti-Semitism was the policy of emerging political parties. In most European nations, the liberals formed political alliances to curb the influence of the church over civil affairs and to limit state support of church institutions, and so made it easy to smear their democratic efforts as a "Jewish conspiracy."

The right of the Jews to civil liberties was taken away during the regime of Hitler in Germany and enabled the lurking anti-Semitism in Europe to allow officially sanctioned murder and stir up the waves of latent and open hatred throughout the world. Unfortunately, historic research has verified that although it started as a political movement, in many countries of Europe, particularly in Germany, anti-Semitism was at least tacitly given church support until church leaders realized that the harvest of hatred was death.

The destructive brutality of Nazism and the establishment of the State of Israel in 1948 overturned traditional Christian portrayals of the Jews as hopeless wanderers and triggered official church reversals of the age-old Christian "teaching" of contempt for Jews. Almost all Christian denominations have recognized that Judaism's covenant with God endures and are engaged in significant interfaith dialogue with Jews. This widespread, honest exchange has never happened before in our shared history.

Yet anti-Semitism still exists in the USA and rears its ugly head with an ever-growing vigor almost throughout the entire known world. But in this new age of rapprochement, such prejudices must not be allowed to jeopardize joint efforts to achieve human freedom for everyone, economic security for the needy and the guarantee of peace for all, both nations and individuals.

A Christian Looks at the Two-Thousand Year Encounter

Philip J. Mayher

Edward Flannery, the Catholic priest who authored *The Anguish of the Jews,* states "The pages that Christians have ripped out of their history books are the ones that the Jews have memorized." To have an adequate dialogue, Christians must acquaint themselves with the long history of anti-Semitic hatred and violence with which Jews are all too familiar. More importantly, we Christians must understand better the impact of the anti-Jewish theology we have written into our books since the earliest days of the church.

The process by which the church separated from the synagogue was long and painful. What is tremendously confusing is that the gospels reflect not only Christianity's Jewish origins and core, but these gospels, written forty to seventy years after the life of Jesus of Nazareth—and at the time of the initial separation of church and synagogue—also reflect the debates and fights that accompanied the beginnings of that separation. Without proper education about the different time frames involved, these argumentative elements can give rise to invalid "anti-Jewish" readings of the texts.

One verse from the Gospel of John illustrates this. The context for John 20:19 is: the Jew Jesus has been crucified by Rome, with the complicity of a Jewish council set up by and beholden to Rome. The scattered Jewish disciples of Jesus have regathered. "When it was evening on that day, the first day of the week, and the doors of the house where the disciples had met were locked *for fear of the Jews,* Jesus came and stood among them and said, 'Peace be with you.'"

This key scripture verse does not say, "The Jewish disciples were hiding for fear of the Romans." It does not even say, "Some Jews were hiding for fear of other Jews." The way John tells it impels the reader, perhaps unwittingly, to view the events from the later situation of the gospel writer rather than from the context of Jesus' ministry decades earlier. Clearly here "the Jews" are the enemy. Why? Because the church community that this Gospel addresses had recently had its Jewish members expelled from the local synagogue (see Jn 9:22; 12:42; 16:2). The anger over this action drives the depiction of "the Jews," the ones who did the expelling, as blind leaders who don't understand what they're doing. The contentious human aspects of the gospel texts can thus be mistakenly interpreted by later readers as universal religious axioms. This is but one instance of such an anti-Jewish potential.

After the New Testament period, in the patristic era, these argumentative passages were supplemented and combined to form an anti-Jewish theology that became imbedded in the Christian tradition. This theology was developed because of the era's social climate, as the church found itself threatened by the vigorous dynamism of Judaism in the Roman world. Its elements add up to what Jules Isaac was the first to call "the teaching of contempt." Isaac memorably characterized three particularly odious and false theological charges leveled by patristic Christianity toward Judaism as the "three Ds": *deicide, dispersion* (or diaspora) and *degeneracy.*

The first charge, *deicide,* blames "*The* Jews" for the killing of Jesus—and by extension, in spite of the theological irrationality of it, somehow thus "killing God." The Jewish people through the centuries have been falsely called "Christ killers," a wrongful opprobrium used to justify violence and mayhem.

The "second D," *dispersion,* claims that, as a consequence for killing Christ, it is God's providential will that the Jews be expelled and dispersed. The first level of patent falseness to this charge is historical. Jews faced persecutorial expulsion from the time of the Exodus to the time of the Babylonian exile— hundreds of years before! Theological bias is being brought to history here, not history to theology! This idea pervaded Western culture, demonstrated by the fact that a common houseplant is still called a "Wandering Jew."

The last of the false charges has perhaps the most currency to this day— *degeneracy.* One view of this charge is that Judaism had become so degenerate by the time of Christ that, again, it was God's will that Christianity replace (supersede) Judaism. The alleged degeneracy of the Pharisees, based on polemics in Christian Scripture, is but one prime instance used to reinforce this charge. But the Pharisees were in actuality hardly a degenerate force— again, quite the contrary! The Pharisees were profound reformers of Judaism. To their teaching is owed a faith in life after death, temple reform, the tradition of Oral Torah, and the bringing of worship into the Jewish home (which alone has enabled Jewish identity to persist through two millennia).

This teaching of contempt, which has been called "bad theology" by Paul

Van Buren and many others, predominated to the Holocaust. Christian theological self-reappraisal since then has resulted in a sea change in the representation of Judaism. In 1965 the Second Vatican Council promulgated the declaration *Nostra Aetate,* which proceeds from the drastically revised premise that "God holds the Jews most dear." In the intervening years almost every major Christian denomination in Europe and the United States has issued a statement rejecting officially any theological teaching which is anti-Jewish. Some, such as my own tradition in the United Church of Christ, have gone so far as to reject any replacement theology outright. Jewish-Christian dialogue has prospered internationally at academic, ecclesiastical and local levels. Extraordinary theological reappraisal is reflected in such works as Paul Van Buren's three-volume *A Theology of the Jewish-Christian Reality* and Clark Williamson's *A Guest in the House of Israel: Post-Holocaust Church Theology,* to name but two of many significant works. A vast project has unfolded before Jews and Christians to replace the enmity of the past with a theological amity that is faithful to the separate but—at least from a Christian point of view—inseparable witnesses of Christianity and Judaism.

Reflection/Discussion Questions

1. What feelings or thoughts come to you when you see a cross or crucifix?
2. What did you find most surprising about these summaries of the history of Jewish and Christian relations? Most disconcerting or upsetting?
3. George Santayana once said that those who forget the past are doomed to repeat it. How would you apply this thought to the relationship between the Christian and Jewish communities?
4. Some Jews and Christians fear interfaith dialogue. Some recall forced conversions that took place in the past or fear assimilation. Others worry about watering down their tradition. What do you think?

Closing Prayer

Leader: The history of our peoples has not been what God would want. Yet now we live in a unique and unprecedented moment of grace. The dialogue between our two communities is more widespread and profound than ever before. Let us pray for those who were the victims of hatred and violence, and dedicate ourselves with greater vigor to the will of God for peace and solidarity.

Mourner's Kaddish

All: Magnified and sanctified be the glory of God
    in the world created according to God's will.
May God's sovereignty soon be acknowledged
    during our lives and the life of Israel and all God's people. Let us say: Amen.
May the glory of God be eternally praised,
    hallowed and extolled, lauded and exalted,
        honored, revered, adored, and worshiped.
Beyond all songs and hymns of exaltation,
    beyond all praise which mortals can utter
        is the glory of the Holy One, praised is the Lord. Let us say: Amen.

Let there be abundant peace from heaven and life's goodness
     for us and for all Israel and for all God's people. Let us say: Amen.
The One who ordains the order of the universe will bring peace
     to us and to all Israel and to all God's people. Let us say: Amen.

SESSION SIX

Making Common Cause:
A Christian's View

Joan Poro

Could it be that the kingdom of God, dearly awaited and prayed for in both traditions, can only arrive when Jews and Christians come together to build it in partnership with their one and same God? I believe this is our common cause, entrusted to us through our distinctive lives-in-covenant with our God.

I come to this belief through my own prayer, participation in interfaith dialogue, study of scripture, and deep sorrow that we have lost the opportunity for such partnership for two millennia. Most important, though, I come to this belief through my day-to-day experience of working in exclusively Christian communities for social change aimed at making this world of ours look more like the kingdom. In these communities, I feel the need to be with our Jewish brothers and sisters.

Let me give an example. For the past couple of years, I have been involved in a small, loosely organized, ecumenical group of clergy and pastoral ministers in the inner city in which I work. We have come together to explore ways in which a coordinated urban ministry might make a difference in the lives of the people in the neighborhood. Our theme comes from the prophet Jeremiah:

Promote the welfare of the city to which I have exiled you; pray for it to the Lord, for upon its welfare depends your own (Jeremiah 29:7).

As we struggle with a Christian response to the concerns expressed by the people in the inner city, I struggle with these questions: If we as Christians feel called by the prophet to work toward the welfare of our city, are not also our

Jewish neighbors? Would not our efforts be stronger and more effective if we worked together in partnership?

It has been more than thirty years since the Second Vatican Council of the Roman Catholic Church issued its watershed *Declaration on the Relationship of the Church to Non-Christian Religions (Nostra Aetate)*. Its statement on relations with the Jews (Section #4) had an immense impact on Protestant churches as well as the Roman Catholic Church, launching a historic era of Christian-Jewish dialogue. The thirtieth anniversary of *Nostra Aetate* (October 1995) was occasion for celebrating the spectacular strides that have been made by church officials and leading rabbis, by professional theologians and by people of both faith traditions at the grass-roots level.

Sharing Shalom is a model for the kind of local interfaith dialogue that has begun to correct misinformation, to destroy stereotypes and to foster greater understanding and appreciation among people of our two traditions. Certainly none of the subjects of the *Sharing Shalom* curriculum could be exhausted in an evening's conversation. But it is my hope that exploring increasingly complex areas of difference, with faithfulness to the process, can help dialogue partners to build a certain level of understanding, appreciation, friendliness and trust. My concern is, what happens at the end of the sixth session?

I would hope it is not the end. The work toward the kingdom has just begun. This is not the time to shake hands and wish one another, "Shalom," and go our separate ways once again.

Continued dialogue grounded in prayer and shared scripture study, can serve to point out that for both faiths the moral imperatives of peace, justice and love are the heart of God's plan for creation. It is time to move beyond dialogue about our differences into discovery of our shared vision:

> Attentive to the same God who has spoken, hanging on the same word, we have to witness to the one same memory and one common hope in him who is the master of history. We must also accept our responsibility to prepare the world for social justice, respect for the rights of persons and nations and for social and international reconciliation. To this we are driven, Jews and Christians, by the command to love our neighbor, by a common hope for the kingdom of God and by the great heritage of the prophets. (Vatican Commission for Religious Relations with Jews, "Notes on the Correct Way to Present Jews and Judaism in Preaching and Catechesis in the Roman Catholic Church" [1985], #11)

Thirty years of renewed relationship is not a long time to heal the wounds of two thousand years of division. But another way of looking at time is to recognize how much we have lost. In the words of Rabbi Leon Klenicki, it is time for going beyond guilt and nonguilt and it is time for addressing together the evil in our world. In two thousand years, Rabbi Klenicki asks, how effective have our religions been in bettering human life? How effective are our religions in bettering the communities in which we live? How are we called to work together to prepare our world for a kingdom of peace, justice and love? These are the questions for continuing dialogue—and making common cause.

Making Common Cause:
A Global Jewish View

Norman Abelson

My friend Joe is blind. He has been blind for all of his eighty-five years. My friend Marcus is gay. My friend Kathi is a woman. My friend Bill is a conservative Republican. My tenants Maggie and Wil are fundamentalist Christians. My friend Phil is Catholic. My doctor is Protestant. Frank is homeless. My brother lives in a state school for the mentally retarded. My friend Steve is a twenty-nine-year-old teacher. Mel and I have known each other for thirty plus years. He is black. I sit as a member of the advisory board for the Salvation Army. My dear old friend Harry is an atheist. My buddy Walter is a Lutheran pastor. Bob is a gay United Church of Christ minister. Sweet Karen is a recent divorcee. Eva is a socialist. And Julie is ill with cancer.

What have all these statements to do with making common cause? Just everything. For I believe, as much as I believe anything, that if each of us got to know one person of every group different from us, hatred and bigotry and scapegoating would disappear. Seem like a miracle? Hardly. Rather, I see it as the single most pragmatic approach to the enormous challenge of learning to live together—peacefully and comfortably.

Let me take you back in time more than fifty years to an industrial city outside Boston. It is the mid-1940s, and a young boy is making his way to Hebrew school one afternoon. He walks fast, hugging the inside of the sidewalk to make himself less visible. But it doesn't work. He hears the familiar yell, "Hey, Jew boy, wait up." He knows it is the boy with the ugly green teeth and his little band of toughs.

Soon he is pinned down, the boy with the dirty teeth sitting on his chest, hitting him and repeating: "The damn Jews have all the money." They tire of the

78

game and let the boy go on his way, calling after him, "Heil Hitler, Jew. Heil Hitler." The boy is traumatized for years by these experiences: it is not until a long time afterward that he is able to consider it rationally and decide what to do about it.

Of course, the boy was me. And for years I have wished that somehow I could bump into the boy with the green teeth—like me, an aging man by now, and tell him this: "If only we had known each other better, or if our parents were friends, it would have been different. While you, in your poverty, were hitting me for being rich, my father was working on a city garbage truck for eight dollars a week. If only we had known each other, I could have explained who Hitler was and what he was doing to kids like us who were Jewish and, in some cases, Catholic like you. If only we had played tag together and shared dreams, like I did with my closest friend, Charlie Perry, a Christian like you, we could have formed an alliance against the rich and greedy people who were keeping us down. If only...."

I never did get to meet that kid again, but I pledged to work to break through the hatred and intolerance I believe is not born into anyone, but is bred—to some degree—into each of us. But before we can reach our exalted goal, we must have the courage to look at ourselves and our own biases and wash them away. It is fairly easy to do this intellectually, since clearly prejudice is a social and religious and moral and ethical flaw. But that is not enough; we must move from the thinking of the mind to the feeling of the heart. There is a Hebrew word: *rachmonis,* compassion, moving a step beyond sympathy to empathy...to an understanding of the pain that hatred causes...to a sharing of that pain...to the joy of discovery that we really all are both different and alike...to the understanding that we can live with our differences if we learn to live and work together and even to love each other for those universal things we hold in common.

The real differences in this world are not the language we speak or what faith we practice or what color we are; rather they are the social and economic injustices that divide people from people, race from race, economic classes from each other. These are the areas in which we must work. If we *have* to hate something, let it be poverty and child hunger and homelessness and war and the use of ethnicity or religion or wealth as reasons for superiority over others. We should not use as a way to feel morally superior, for example, a fourteen-year-old minority ghetto girl with a child of her own, who is uneducated, downtrodden and frightened to death. Such feelings are inhuman and will only serve to separate us more, turning our hearts to stone.

We must learn the best that our religions preach, and practice those things, because, after all, it is the act that counts. How do we make common cause?

First, by a recognition of our shared humanity, complete with its foibles and weaknesses as well as its ability to transcend and seek a higher purpose. For if we profess a belief in something bigger and better than we, something to reach for, then surely it is a blasphemy of the highest order not to live together in respect and even affection. I believe that is the closest we can come to God.

Reflection/Discussion Questions

1. Thinking back over the past six weeks, what things have been the most significant for you?
2. What are some things that Christianity and Judaism hold in common? In what ways do they differ?
3. What have you learned about your own faith tradition that was new to you?
4. What should happen now?

Closing Prayer

Leader: We have come to the end, at least for now, of our time of interfaith dialogue. We have learned more about how we understand our faiths, our celebrations, our traditions, our history and our duty to work together as partners in God's plan. God seems to have wanted to promote partnerships right from the very beginning, as this story makes clear:

"Partners" by Marc Gellman (see page 108)

Leader: I would invite anyone who would wish to say a few words about partnership and interfaith dialogue to do so now.

Time for Sharing

Leader: Let us conclude our time together with a Jewish prayer for the coming of God's kingdom that closely parallels the "Our Father" prayer, which is dear to all Christians:

May the time not be distant, O God, when Your name shall be worshiped in all the earth, when unbelief shall disappear and error shall be no more. Fervently we pray that the day may come when all shall turn to You in love, when corruption and evil shall give way to integrity and goodness, when superstition shall no longer enslave the mind, nor idolatry blind the eye, when all who dwell on earth shall know that You alone are God. O may all, created in Your image, become one in spirit and one in friendship, for ever united in your service. Then shall Your kingdom be established on earth, and the word of Your prophet fulfilled, "The Lord will reign for ever and ever." Amen.
—from *Gates of Prayer: The New Union Prayerbook* (1975).

APPENDIX 1:
TEXTUAL SUPPLEMENT

An Outline of the Rabbinic Writings

Arthur F. Starr

The basis of Jewish Law is, at the very outset, the scriptural or written Torah. Perhaps more than anything else, though, it was the *Mishnah* and the *Talmud* that allowed Judaism to survive outside of the Land of Israel through the adaptation of Jewish religious experience to the demands of life in the context of a non-Jewish world. In addition to being the source and basis of modern Jewish Law, the *Talmud* also provides insights into the lives of the people who lived at and before the time of its writing through the legends and lore that it contains.

The *Mishnah,* compiled and edited at the beginning of the third century, is a collection of laws and ethics. The *Mishnah* represents and is the foundation of the Oral Law, handed down through the generations, which retains Divine Authority along with the Written Law, the Torah. The authorities quoted in the *Mishnah* are the *Tannaim,* the religious teachers, who followed the prophets and lasted until the end of the second century C.E., a period of about five hundred years.

The *Gemara* are texts that amplify the *Mishnah.* In a broad sense, the *Mishnah* and *Gemara* together make up the *Talmud* or Oral Law. More specifically, within the category of *Gemara* are two *Talmuds:* the *Yerushalmi,* or the Talmud of the Land of Israel, probably composed in Tiberias in Galilee around 300–400 C.E., and the Babylonian Talmud or *Bavli,* composed in Babylon around 500–600 C.E.. Both discussed the *Mishnah* and its scriptural basis in the Torah, but the *Bavli* joined Torah and *Mishnah* together more thoroughly. Jews for centuries have, therefore, approached the written Law, the Torah, by way of the Oral Law, and most especially through the *Bavli.*

Both the *Mishnah* and the *Talmud* are arranged in six parts, or orders, and are composed of sixty-three tractates. A listing of the six orders and their component tractates follows:

1. *Zera'im* deals with laws relating to agriculture, contains eleven tractates including one on blessings and prayers.

   a. *Berachoth*—deals with blessings and prayers, liturgy, etc.

   b. *Peah*—laws concerning the gleaning of the corners of the field.

   c. *Demmai*—treatment of corn that has not been tithed.

   d. *Kilayim*—discusses prohibited mixtures (animals, garments, etc.)

   e. *Shebiith*—laws of the Sabbatical year.

   f. *Terumoth*—types of required offerings.

   g. *Maasroth*—discusses tithes given to the Levites.

   h. *Maaser Sheni*—the second required tithe.

   i. *Challah*—deals with the portion of dough to be given to the priests.

   j. *Orlah*—laws relating to new fruit trees.

   k. *Bikkurim*—deals with the subject of the first fruits that were to be brought to the Temple.

2. *Mo'ed* contains twelve tractates dealing with festivals and *Shabbat,* including a discussion of what is considered work prohibited on *Shabbat.*

   a. *Shabbat*—laws dealing with the *Sabbath.*

   b. *Erubim*—boundaries regulated by *Shabbat.*

   c. *Pesachim*—laws dealing with Passover.

   d. *Shekalim*—deals with the annual tax to be paid to the Temple.

   e. *Yoma*—laws of the Day of Atonement.

   f. *Sukkah*—laws of Succoth, the Feast of Tabernacles.

   g. *Betzah*—laws dealing with work permitted on the Festivals.

   h. *Rosh Hashshanah*—New Year explanations and rules.

   i. *Taanith*—regulations relating to Fast Days.

   j. *Megillah*—regulations concerning the reading of the Scroll of Esther on Purim.

   k. *Moed Katan*—regulations concerning the intermediary days of the Festivals.

   l. *Chagigah*—details of private offerings on the Festivals.

3. *Nashim* deals with laws of marriage and divorce and has seven tractates.

   a. *Yebamoth*—laws of the Levirite Marriage.

   b. *Ketuboth*—details of marriage contracts.

   c. *Nedarim*—concerning vows that are taken and their annulment.

   d. *Nazir*—concerning the vows of the Nazirite.

   e. *Sotah*—laws dealing with adultery.

   f. *Gittin*—divorce laws and regulations.

   g. *Kiddushin*—laws relating to marriage.

4. *Nezikin* has ten tractates dealing with civil law.
   a. *Baba Kamma*—treats the subject of damages and injuries.
   b. *Baba Metzia*—laws concerning property that was found.
   c. *Baba Bathra*—deals with regulations of real estate and commerce.
   d. *Sanhedrin*—deals with courts of law.
   e. *Maccoth*—the punishment for false witnesses.
   f. *Shevuoth*—types of oaths, private and public.
   g. *Eduyoth*—traditional laws and testimonies of distinguished rabbis.
   h. *Avodah Zara*—laws concerning idolatry.
   i. *Avoth*—ethical statements of the rabbis.
   j. *Horayoth*—deals with following erroneous decisions by the authorities.

5. *Kodashim* consists of eleven tractates dealing mostly with sacrifices in the Temple.
   a. *Zevachim*—animal sacrifices.
   b. *Menachoth*—meal and drink offerings.
   c. *Chullin*—proper slaughtering of animals and the dietary laws.
   d. *Bechoroth*—laws of the firstborn (animals and man).
   e. *Arachin*—how to evaluate things dedicated by a vow to God so they can be redeemed.
   f. *Themurah*—laws concerning sanctified things that have been exchanged.
   g. *Kerithoth*—how to expiate the punishment of excision.
   h. *Meilah*—punishments for profaning sacred things.
   i. *Tamid*—laws of the daily offerings in the Temple.
   j. *Middoth*—laws of measurement.
   k. *Kinnim*—deals with laws concerning the offering of birds.

6. *Tohoroth* has twelve tractates dealing with ritual purity.
   a. *Kelim*—vessels that have been defiled.
   b. *Ohaloth*—ritually unclean homes because of a dead body.
   c. *Negaim*—laws relating to leprosy.
   d. *Parah*—purification with the ashes of the Red Heifer.
   e. *Teharoth*—defilements that end at sunset.
   f. *Mikvaoth*—ritual baths.
   g. *Nidah*—menstruation laws.
   h. *Machshirin*—liquids that can defile.
   i. *Zavim*—uncleanness caused by bloody issues.
   j. *Tebul Yom*—immersion and purification at sunset.
   k. *Yadayim*—how to purify hands that have been defiled.
   l. *Uktzin*—stalks and shells that can defile.

An Outline of the Christian New Testament

Philip A. Cunningham

The Christian Bible consists of two parts: all the books of the *Tanakh*, or Hebrew Scriptures, comprise the first part, although they are arranged in a different order. Some denominations include a small number of additional books in this first part. The second part are the specifically Christian Scriptures, usually known as the New Testament. All Christian denominations hold that the New Testament contains the same twenty-seven books.

There are basically four types of literature represented by these twenty-seven books. The four Gospels are narratives that relate the life, death and resurrection of Jesus. One book, the Acts of the Apostles, narrates the origins and spreading of the church. Twenty-one epistles or letters are messages sent to early church communities by apostles, disciples of apostles, or other churches. The last book, Revelation, is an apocalyptic book similar to the Book of Daniel in the Hebrew Scriptures. It uses highly symbolic and imaginative language to speak of the ultimate triumph of good over evil.

Jesus of Nazareth conducted a public ministry which resulted in his execution by the Romans, probably in the year 30 C.E. All of the present New Testament books were written roughly between the years 50 and 110 C.E. With the exception of Paul of Tarsus, little is known about the authors of most of these books since many were written anonymously or pseudonymously. In the case of the Gospels, for example, the names they now bear were applied to them over a century after their composition.

Here is a brief outline of these twenty-seven books in the order in which they appear in the New Testament. The approximate dates of their composition that will be indicated represent a widespread consensus among those Christian denominations, including Roman Catholic, Episcopal, Lutheran, Methodist, United Church of Christ, American Baptist and others, which study the Bible using historical-critical analysis. Because they present the story of Jesus, the four Gospels are given priority in the New Testament.

I. The Gospels

A. The Gospel of Matthew tells the story of Jesus from his infancy until his resurrection. The author presents a very Jewish picture of Jesus as one who epitomizes Torah life and teaches God's Way with divine authority. The Gospel was probably written between 80–90 C.E. The writer seems to have had some form of the Gospel of Mark in his possession.

B. The Gospel of Mark was likely written in a church community that had experienced some severe trauma, probably persecution. The narrative about Jesus, which begins with his baptism as an adult by John the Baptizer in the River Jordan, emphasizes that God was revealed in Jesus' suffering and that followers of Jesus can expect to encounter suffering, too. It likely was written around the year 70 C.E.

C. The Gospel of Luke begins the story of Jesus with dual annunciations of the imminent births of John the Baptizer and of Jesus. Apparently written with a Gentile audience in mind, Jesus is portrayed as the bringer of healing, peace, and reconciliation. Like Matthew's, this Gospel was also likely written between 80–90 C.E., and its author also seems to have had access to the Gospel of Mark.

D. The Gospel of John of all the four is the one most influenced by Greek philosophical ideas. The story of Jesus begins before the creation of the world. Jesus is understood as one who descends into the human world from the realm of God above, reveals God and shares eternal life with those who accept his divine origins, and returns home to his Father by being "lifted up" in crucifixion/resurrection. Probably written in the 90s C.E., this Gospel vividly manifests the growing separation between the church and Judaism.

II. Acts

The Acts of the Apostles is a companion volume to the Gospel of Luke and was in all probability composed by the same author in the mid-80s C.E. It tells a stylized story of the spread of the church out from Jerusalem into Samaria and out into the Gentile world. The first half focuses on the difficult decision to admit Gentiles into the community, while the second features Paul of Tarsus evangelizing throughout the eastern Mediterranean, ending with him preaching freely in the capital of the known world—Rome.

III. Epistles

A. The Pauline Epistles consist of thirteen letters either written or dictated by Paul of Tarsus himself or composed posthumously in his name, a typical practice of the time, by disciples who wished to perpetuate his mission. Paul probably was executed during the persecution of Christians in Rome by Caesar Nero, 64–66 C.E. Denominations that used historical-critical methods to interpret the Bible understand the letters asterisked below to have been written by Paul himself between the years 50–60 C.E. 1 Thessalonians is widely believed to have been composed around 50 C.E., and so is both the earliest Pauline letter and the earliest New Testament book. Romans is thought by many scholars to be the last letter Paul wrote. The final four epistles listed below are all addressed to individuals. All the others are addressed to local Gentile churches founded by Paul (except for Romans) and are identified by the city or region in which they are located.

1. **Romans***—thought by many to be the most thoughtful of Paul's letters, it seeks to present his understanding of the Good News of Jesus in an orderly way so as to introduce Paul to this important church which he plans to eventually visit.
2. **1 Corinthians***—addressed to an extremely busy seaport, both Corinthian letters try to deal with excesses in the understanding of the Good News by Gentiles.
3. **2 Corinthians***
4. **Galatians***—Paul's angriest letter in which he seeks to correct superstitious understandings about entry into the church.
5. **Ephesians**—a meditation on the divine plan of God, brought to fruition in Christ, by which Gentiles along with Jews are being brought into the Church—metaphorically understood as the Body of Christ and the Bride of Christ.
6. **Philippians***—partially an angry response to confusion about whether Gentiles in the church should be circumcised, the letter contains a profound reflection on the meaning of Christ's death.
7. **Colossians**—a mystical consideration on the cosmic significance of Christ who brings the church into the world of God even while it is still experiencing earthly existence.
8. **1 Thessalonians***—a letter in which Paul effusively praises what may have been his first successful Gentile church. He also addresses a pastoral crisis brought about by the delay in the expected return of Christ in glory.

9. **2 Thessalonians**—reiterates many of the themes of 1 Thessalonians, with more attention paid to some sort of persecution being experienced in that community.
10. **1 Timothy**—this and the next two letters are often referred to as the "Pastoral Epistles." They were all probably written near the end of the first century C.E. They reflect a time of developing church structures and offices, discussing, for example, the qualifications of bishops and deacons. They also seek to deal with the threat of various heresies which are appearing.
11. **2 Timothy**
12. **Titus**
13. **Philemon***—in this letter Paul returns a slave named Onesimus to his master, Philemon. Both are now members of the church and Paul urges Philemon to accept Onesimus as a brother in Christ.

B. General Epistles: All of the following epistles were written in the last third of the first century C.E. Their authorship, addressees and specific situations cannot be readily determined.

1. **Hebrews**—offers a theological reflection on the significance of Christ using the image of the Jewish Temple priesthood. Christ is seen as the eternal high priest whose sinless self-sacrifice does away with the need for any other forms of ritual atonement.
2. **James**—is usually regarded as a very Jewish series of reflections on the necessity of putting one's faith into concrete action. The attribution to James, "the brother of the Lord," adds to the Jewish, as opposed to Greek, tonality of the letter.
3. **1 Peter**—seemingly addressed to recent converts, this letter emphasizes that they have been brought into a holy people and exhorts them to live holy lives. Despite the Petrine attribution, it and 2 Peter are widely felt to have been composed toward the end of the first century C.E.
4. **2 Peter**—deals with a false teaching about the return of Christ in glory and judgment.
5. **1 John**—the three Johannine letters all seem to come from the same community in which the Gospel of John was composed, written after the Gospel toward the end of the first century C.E. They reflect fragmenting communities, divided by theological differences, seeking to hold on to an essential teaching from the Gospel of John: disciples of Jesus must love one another.
6. **2 John**
7. **3 John**

8. **Jude**—a very short sermon that urges readers to be faithful to the teachings of the apostles and not to be misled by heretical ideas.

IV. Apocalyptic

Revelation—probably written around 95 C.E., this is a highly symbolic exhortation to churches suffering under a Roman persecution in Asia Minor during the reign of the Caesar Domitian. Christians are assured that the wicked will be destroyed when Christ establishes God's "new heaven and new earth" in all their fullness. They must, therefore, not succumb to threats of torture and death, but remain steadfast in their faith.

APPENDIX 2:
LEADERS' GUIDE

Suggestions for Organization and Facilitation

Getting Started

It has been our experience that a process such as *Sharing Shalom* works best when it is hosted by leaders in synagogues or churches or academic institutions relatively near to one another. Ideally, rabbis, ministers, priests or other congregational leaders should be active participants if not the actual hosts. They can be on hand to welcome participants, facilitate small groups, introduce the sessions' topics and offer guidance when there is uncertainty about some teaching in one or the other tradition.

When a collaborative decision is made to conduct *Sharing Shalom,* a schedule for the six sessions must be agreed upon. We recommend that they occur on consecutive days or weeks so as to maintain continuity and build momentum. Be sure to take both Christian and Jewish holy days into account. Advertising can then begin within the participating communities.

Registration in advance is a necessity for several reasons. A fairly accurate participant count is needed to order guidebooks, to arrange for the facilitation of the number of small groups that will be required, and to try to maintain some parity between the numbers of Jewish and Christian participants. In order for a true dialogue to take place, there should be as close to an equal number of Christians and Jews as possible. If it happens that there is one Jew for every two Christians, then the dynamics begin to change from an equal dialogue to a question-and-answer session directed at the minority group. On your registration form, there should be a space for the participants to indicate their religious affiliation. Care should also be taken to balance Protestant, Catholic and Orthodox Christian participation.

In the promotional materials, it should be stressed that a six-session commitment is being requested. Frequent absences will negatively affect the interpersonal dynamics of each small group and disrupt the gradual building of trust and openness that should be building from session to session.

There are two special categories of persons who may be attracted to this sort of interfaith dialogue. Persons who are themselves married or who have relatives who are married to a member of the other tradition will frequently find this

95

an appealing opportunity to learn more about the other religion in a safe and welcoming environment. Provided that the discussions do not deviate to the particular concerns of trying to live out an interfaith marriage, their involvement in the process should be beneficial because of their high degree of motivation. A small group consisting of people in this circumstance might be helpful if the small group facilitator has experience in their characteristic issues.

Another potentially interested person is someone who has converted from Judaism to Christianity and considers him/herself to be a "messianic Jew." Such people often have a proselytizing agenda which would disrupt or sidetrack the main purpose of interfaith dialogue between Christians and Jews. The complex interpersonal dynamics that they would create could be quite upsetting. The hosts and organizers of the process must be very confident that a certain individuals with this background would not advance their own campaign before accepting their registration.

Once registrations have been collected, *Sharing Shalom* books would need to be distributed to all participants before the first gathering. These could be picked up at participating churches or synagogues. Participants should be sorted in advance into small groups for the actual conversations. The ideal number of people in each small group is around ten, not including the facilitator. Again, there should be as close to an equal number of Jews and Christians as possible. We recommend that people stay in the same groupings for all six sessions. With shifting group compositions, a new group identity and comfort level must be reestablished each time. Name badges displaying name and small group number or color code should be prepared and used each session. A master list of participants and group assignments should be prepared and distributed to all facilitators at the first session.

The meeting space itself is important. Ideally, there should be a large space to accommodate all participants for the opening and closing of each session. Small groups would be most at ease in smaller, separate rooms where their conversation will not interfere with the other groups.

Finally, it would be beneficial for the hosts and facilitators to meet before the first session to become better acquainted with one another and with the process. They might meet briefly after each session for a review of the conversation and to plan for the next gathering.

The Agenda for Each Session

If the total number of participants is large enough (i.e., roughly sixteen people) to break into small groups, we recommend that each session open and close with a total group gathering. The optional opening activities that follow could be adapted to fit the particular circumstances. Alternatively, the hosts could begin with opening remarks to set the topic for the session before the participants break up into their small groups. If the personnel resources are available, various presenters could begin with their own brief reflections on the session's theme to complement the *Sharing Shalom* essays in order to spark the conversation.

We have found that a two-hour time frame works quite well. After a roughly fifteen-minute opening segment (see the optional opening activities), the small groups dialogue for about an hour. It is important that all the small groups keep to the same schedule. A designated timekeeper for the whole process might be beneficial. After a fifteen-minute break for refreshments and socializing, the total group reconvenes for about fifteen minutes for the small groups to summarize quickly the most significant points that occurred. Then the session concludes with the prayer experience provided in this volume. Afterward, all facilitators should meet briefly to share their assessment of the dialogue and to plan for the next session, including any materials that might be needed.

Small-Group Facilitators

The organizers or hosts need to select persons to facilitate the small groups who, ideally, are reliable, experienced, somewhat knowledgeable and connected to their communities. The primary duty of the facilitator is to guide the discussion in such a way as to promote substantive, flowing interaction that includes everyone. The facilitator must resist the temptation to use their position to dominate the conversation. Instead, s/he should strive to create a safe and encouraging atmosphere that welcomes the voicing of people's experiences. A statement about respecting one another's confidences, both between Jews and Christians and within the Christian and Jewish communities themselves, should be made at the outset.

Urge all participants to do the advance reading and to familiarize themselves with the guidelines listed on page 16. The first session should begin with a review of these guidelines after individual introductions have been made. Some of these should be repeated weekly, especially numbers 1, 2 and 5. Encourage the group not to be so cautious about stepping on toes that they refrain from posing sincere questions. Stress that everyone's good intentions are taken for granted and that everyone has come together as Jews and Christians to learn about one another's experiences of God.

The facilitators should use their authority to prevent the monopolization of the discussion by outspoken people. This can be done by simply saying, "I'd like to hear from people who haven't said much yet," or "I wonder what participants from the other religious community think about that." Care should also be taken to avoid the role of the "expert authority" upon whom the group becomes dependent. This can be resisted, for example, by not sitting at the head of a rectangular table.

The dialogue unfolds by discussing each session's reflection/discussion questions. It might begin with the facilitator refreshing everyone's memories about the major points of the essays, using the section, "Comments on Weekly Essays and Discussion," as a guide. The discussion questions are designed to flow together. Do not simply go around the group one by one, but ask, "Does anyone want to offer their thoughts or ideas about this question?" As the conversation ensues, try to include everyone who wishes to speak and see that both Jewish and Christian perspectives are expressed.

If a digression occurs that captures the group's enthusiasm, feel free to "go with the flow" for a time before returning to the questions. Facilitators should be alert to the interest level of participants. If the conversation has taken a turn into an unpopular or exhausted tangent, move on. As the chat about a particular question peters out, or if someone naturally segues into the next question, move on.

If in the course of the exchange, a participant states something that the facilitator knows or strongly suspects to be an erroneous religious statement, and if no one else challenges it, feel free to interject a mild correction. If the speaker is adamant, you might say, "I really don't feel that what you've said is completely accurate. I'll check it out before our next session." The same could be said if a question of information is raised to which no one has an answer. After the session, consult with the organizers or hosts or other authority, and so inform the group at the next session.

As the dialogue time draws to a close, it might be useful to ask the group what struck them as most significant about the exchange. This would serve as the basis for the summary comments that might be made to the total group, if that is how your agenda is organized.

It would be a wise practice to meet briefly after the session with any other small group facilitators to share your assessment of how things went and any improvements that might be made.

Optional Opening Activities

These activities were designed with a total group of about thirty people in mind who would later break up into three small groups. Feel free to modify them in any way to meet your needs.

Session One: Four Corners

Chairs should be arranged in rows in the center of a large the room. In each of the four corners of the room are hanging large signs that read: "Human Being," "American," "Jew or Christian," and "Man or Woman."

Following a welcoming of the group and the introduction of the leaders, people are asked to pick up their chairs and to move IMMEDIATELY (i.e., don't spend time mulling over the decision) to the corner whose answer they most quickly identify with:

1. WHICH TERM BEST IDENTIFIES WHO YOU ARE?
   A human being
   An American
   A Jew or a Christian
   A man or a woman

When the people have congregated in the corners, ask them to introduce themselves to each other. Then ask them to explain to those in their corner why they selected their answer and not any of the others.

2. DIALOGUE GROUPING
After about ten or fifteen minutes, ask the people to pick up their chairs and assemble in the small groups denoted on their name badges. Each small group facilitator will introduce him/herself and ask the others to introduce themselves with their names, towns of residence, religious tradition and why they decided to join this interfaith process.

Session Two: Holiday Questionnaire

As people arrive they can pick up their name tags and gather either as a total group or in their small groups. When everyone has assembled, they are welcomed and asked to complete the form below. It might be wise to have pencils or pens available.

Holiday Questionnaire

Below is a list of major and minor Jewish and Christian observances. Choose one of your tradition's holidays that has particular emotional associations (positive or negative) for you, and complete the table about them. Discuss in your group when done.

——Rosh Hashanah	——Advent
——Yom Kippur	——Christmas
——Sukkot	——Epiphany
——Simchat Torah	——Lent
——Chanukah	——Palm Sunday
——Purim	——Holy or Maundy Thursday
——Passover	——Good Friday
——Yom Hashoah	——Easter
——Israel Independence Day	——Pentecost
——Shavuoth	——A Marian feast: _____
——Tisha B'Av	——A Saint's feast: _____
	——Halloween or All Saints' Day

Holiday Name:	
When I think of this holiday I think of:	
Doing (activities)	
Feelings	
Smelling (aromas)	
Special memories	

Session Three: Forced Choice

Opening Activity:

After arrival, participants are organized into their small groups. The facilitator passes to each person in the group a page on which the following multiple choice statement is printed.

Prayer is: A. A way for me to communicate with and influence God.

                B. A way for me to change myself through reflection or contemplation.

                C. A way for a community to express its gratitude, hopes and fears.

                D. A way for God to speak to me.

Participants are asked to select, as spontaneously as possible, which of the four responses they most prefer by circling it. Ask for a show of hands for each of the responses. Then ask for anyone to explain or elaborate upon their choice. Defer any suggestions for modifications of the phrasing of the options until the end of the discussion. As people speak, see if any patterns among the religious denominations or traditions are emerging. After the conversation has unfolded for about fifteen minutes, thank the group for their comments and turn its attention to the subject of weekly worship services. Consider the Reflection/Discussion Questions for Session Three.

Session Four: Word Association

After the participants have assembled in either the total or small dialogue groups, they are to write down the first word that comes into their minds when they hear each of the following words announced:

Peace
Love
Kindness
Fellowship
Promise

When all five words have been considered, participants are asked to share their responses with one another. When this has been done, the facilitator will ask the group to react to the question: "Do you think these words have any connection to a messianic Age to Come?"

After discussing this, the conversation will turn to the Reflection/Discussion Questions for Session Four.

Session Five: Object Association

Advanced Preparation:
The following or similar objects will be needed for this week's opening activity:

1. A red or white yarmulke
2. Rosary beads
3. A phylactery or a mezuzah
4. A Bible (preferably a large, family-style one)
5. A crucifix or a cross

Opening Activity:
After a welcoming, the participants assemble in their dialogue groups. If possible, the lights in the meeting area might be dimmed somewhat. The objects for reflection should be hidden in a bag or in some other way. The facilitator explains that after participants close their eyes, objects will be passed around the circle. They can travel in both directions around the circle. With their eyes closed, participants should feel the objects and try to discern what they are. They may open their eyes after a while before passing each object along. Participants are asked to examine each object, but not to make verbal comments.

After all the objects have circulated, the facilitator will ask what people thought as they saw the various objects. Save the discussion on the crucifix or cross until the last as a segue into the Reflection/Discussion Questions for Session 5. Be aware that some Jews have negative associations with this Christian symbol. Hopefully, such feelings will be expressed. The facilitator could then observe that symbols generate different meanings to different people according to how they have been experienced. Whether one experiences history as part of a majority or minority group will shape their feelings toward the symbols of the other group.

Session Six: Four Corners

Advanced Preparation:
In each corner of the meeting room, the following four signs should be hung:

GAP BETWEEN RICH AND POOR

INTOLERANCE

MORAL DECAY

VIOLENCE

Opening Activity:

After gathering as a total group, participants are asked to make an instanta-
neous response to the following question by taking their chairs to the appropriate corner.

"Which issue do you think it is most important that Jews and Christians
immediately begin to address?"

Once gathered in the corners, facilitators will ask the participants to explain
why they chose their response and what they think Jews and Christians should
do about the issue. After the discussion has unfolded for about fifteen minutes,
ask the groups to reassemble in their small dialogue groups and begin convers-
ing about the Reflection/Discussion Questions for Session Six.

Comments on Weekly Essays and Discussions

Session One

The essays for this session offer the perspectives of one Jew and one Christian on what their faith means to them. David G. Stahl, a past synagogue president and dentist, emphasizes Judaism's concern for justice, charity, righteousness and personal study. Louise Mann, an Episcopal priest, discusses the variety of Christian denominations and the importance for Christians of following Jesus Christ in preparing for God's kingdom through prayer, worship and service.

During the discussion on these essays it is likely that someone will express the idea that Judaism tends to define itself as a culture or a people who are supposed to act as God desires, while Christianity tends to think of itself as a religion to which people commit themselves and which is more concerned than Judaism about beliefs and doctrines. Care should be taken not to draw these distinctions too starkly since both approaches can be found among the variety of movements and denominations in both traditions.

Session Two

For this meeting, Claire G. Metzger, a Jewish cantor, and Ellen Zucker, a Jewish educator, have provided an overview of the most important Jewish religious festivals: *Rosh Hashanah, Yom Kippur, Sukkot, Pesaḥ, Shavuot* and the Sabbath. Paul R. Demers, a vowed member of a Catholic men's religious community, offers the same for the Christian seasons and feasts of Advent, Christmas, Lent and Easter.

Combined with the next session, this topic provides a perfect opportunity to gather in one another's houses of worship. Brief tours of the synagogue or church would augment the essays beautifully.

During the dialogue of this session, participants will share personal memories of celebrating these holy days. Particular ethnic practices will likely be

described by both Christians and Jews. Similarities and differences will naturally be perceived as the two traditions are compared. The fourth question
moves the discussion to Jews and Christians together looking out at contemporary American society.

Session Three

Continuing from the last session's look at religious feasts and seasons, this
week's essays provide an overview of typical Jewish and Christian Sabbath
worship. Arthur F. Starr, a Reform rabbi, and Barbara Anne Radtke, a Catholic
theology professor, describe the essential features of the weekend services of
the four main Jewish movements and of the various Christian denominations.

This session, combined with the previous one, provides a good opportunity
to meet in one another's houses of worship. Specific objects in the synagogue
or church could be linked to the session's essays.

In the dialogue, there may be a tendency to harmonize overly or to syn-
cretize Jewish and Christian worship. Since Christian worship forms developed out of Jewish rituals, there are some marked similarities in modern
worship. The modern Conservative and Reform movements in Judaism have
also been heavily influenced by Christian practice. However, the Jesus-centered prayers of Christians is a major difference between the two communities
that should not be minimized.

Session Four

In this session, Philip A. Cunningham, a Catholic theology professor, and
Arthur F. Starr, a Reform rabbi, explore the complex history of messianic
expectations. Their main points are: (1) at the time of Jesus there was an enormous diversity of Jewish speculation about messiah(s), none of which
included a suffering figure; (2) Christians reinterpreted Hebrew expectations
in the light of Jesus and so narrowed and redefined "messiah"; while the rabbis
also narrowed Jewish definitions in partial response to Christian claims; and
(3) even though today Jews and Christians operate with different definitions of
messiah, both communities believe that God wants them to help prepare the
world for a "messianic age" of universal justice and peace.

The differences in messianic understanding will probably come as a surprise
to both Christian and Jewish participants. Christians will be confronted with the
reality that God's kingdom is not fully present in our world, and Jews will be
challenged by the Christian idea that in some preliminary or anticipatory way,

God's kingdom has begun to emerge. Stress the importance of Jews and Christians respecting one another's differing emphases and self-definitions.

Session Five

Joel Klein, a Conservative rabbi and practicing psychotherapist, and Philip J. Mayher, a pastor and educator in the United Church of Christ, both treat the history of Jewish and Christian relations. Klein presents a factual historical outline, while Mayher sketches the "three Ds" of the perennial Christian teaching against Jews in terms of deicide, dispersion and degeneracy.

Most Christians are shocked and dismayed to learn this history, and feelings of shame or guilt often arise. They are often stunned to learn that Christian religious symbols can produce negative emotional responses in Jews because of this history. Jews may be surprised at Christian lack of historical awareness and may be made uncomfortable by their colleagues' efforts to cope with this new knowledge. They will also have to deal with internal and external perceptions as perpetual victims.

Encourage a recognition that the past can only be healed by confronting it and moving beyond it to a new relationship. Discussion on question 3 could be furthered by asking participants to reflect on the origins of tensions between the synagogue and the church. Question 4 is meant to lead to consideration of the steps needed to build a new and positive relationship.

Session Six

Joan Poro, a Catholic pastoral minister and educator, and Norman Abelson, a Jewish writer and social activist, each are concerned with moving beyond dialogue to collaborative Christian and Jewish service to society at large. They ask: What things could and should we be doing together?

This question might be a good one with which to begin this session's dialogue. From it, the Reflection/Discussion Questions move to a review of the entire six-week process. *Sharing Shalom* can serve as the foundation for ongoing interfaith activities in your community. This session's conversation might be an occasion for advanced, yet concrete planning in this regard. Move the discussion gradually from personal considerations to the more communal question, "What should happen now?"

Partners

A Story about Creation *by Marc Gellman*

(For use in closing prayer for Session Six)

Before there was anything, there was God, a few angels, and a huge swirling glob of rocks and water with no place to go. The angels asked God, "Why don't you clean up this mess?"

So God collected rocks from the huge swirling glob and put them together in clumps and said, "Some of these clumps of rocks will be planets, and some will be stars, and some of these rocks will be…just rocks." Then the angels said, "Well God, it's neater now, but is it finished?" and God answered… "NOPE!"

On some rocks God placed growing things, and creeping things, and things that only God knows what they are, and when God had done all this, the angels asked God, "Is the world finished now?" And God answered: "NOPE!"

God made a man and a woman from some of the water and dust and said to them, "I am tired now. Please finish up the world for me…really, it's almost done." But the man and the woman said, "We can't finish the world alone! You have the plans and we are too little."

"You are big enough," God answered them. "But I agree to this. If you keep trying to finish the world, I will be your partner."

The man and the woman asked, "What's a partner?" and God answered, "A partner is someone you work with on a big thing that neither of you can do alone. If you have a partner, it means that you can never give up, because your partner is depending on you. On the days you think I am not doing enough and on the days I think you are not doing enough, even on those days we are still partners and we must not stop trying to finish the world. That's the deal." And they all agreed to that deal.

Then the angels asked God, "Is the world finished yet?" and God answered, "I don't know. Go ask my partners."

From Marc Gellman, *Does God Have a Big Toe? Stories about Stories in the Bible* (New York: Harper & Row, 1989).

APPENDIX 3:
FOR MORE INFORMATION

Glossary

B.C.E./C.E. are alternatives to the Western practice of naming the historical epochs that do not presuppose faith in Christ and hence are more appropriate for interfaith dialogue than the conventional B.C./A.D. They stand for *Before the Common Era* and *Common Era.*

Christ is the Greek form of the Hebrew word *mashiach,* or *messiah,* and literally means an "anointed one." The Hebrew and Greek forms no longer have identical meanings. For Christians, Jesus Christ is the one whom God anointed as the inaugurator of God's Reign, but whose messianic tasks will not be completed until his return in glory when the Reign will be established in all its fullness.

Covenant, from the Hebrew word *b'rith,* is an agreement between parties, especially that between God and Israel, or later, between God and the church through Jesus Christ. In these religious senses, covenant is more than just a contractual agreement. It is a sharing in life together with mutual duties and obligations.

Ecumenical refers to the movement toward collaboration and unity among the diverse Christian communities. It has become especially influential in the twentieth century.

Hebrew Scriptures are the sacred books of Israel. Jews refer to them as *Tanakh,* an acronym for the Hebrew divisions of Teachings *(Torah),* Prophets *(Nevi'im)* and Writings *(Kethuvim).* Christians also consider these books to be sacred, although they arrange their order differently. Christians have traditionally referred to them as the Old Testament, a term which many Jews find offensive because it can promote a triumphalist attitude among Christians. In recent years various alternative names have been offered. Perhaps "Shared Testament" would be an appropriate way for Christians to refer to these texts as a reminder of the ongoing spiritual vitality of Judaism.

Kingdom of God or **Reign of God** is the metaphor used by Jesus to speak of the Age to Come or New Creation. Conceptually rooted in the Hebrew Torah and prophetic tradition, it refers to the inevitable destiny of everything that exists to conform to God's will. Then the lion will lie down with the lamb, the swords will be beaten into plowshares, universal shalom and justice will prevail and all people will acknowledge the Lordship of the God of Israel.

Sacrament is a ritual action through which God's presence can be discerned. All Christians acknowledge baptism and eucharist as sacraments, but some denominations consider other rituals to be sacraments as well. The Roman Catholic tradition, for example, has seven sacraments.

Shalom is a Hebrew word that has many layers of meaning. It means peace, wholeness and right relationship.

Tikkun Olam is a Hebrew expression that means "mend the world." It relates to the covenantal obligation to be partners with God in bringing creation to its divinely intended completion.

Trinity refers to the Christian understanding that God is intrinsically relational, even in God's own being. God is Source, Creator, Sustainer or Father of all that exists, who eternally generates the Revealing Word, Wisdom or Son through which all things are made and are made comprehensible, and whose creative and irrepressible Spirit animates, inspires and draws all things to God. Christians also believe that God's Word, God's revealing self, was incarnate in Jesus, a first-century Galilean Jew.

A Brief Annotated Bibliography

The following works may be of assistance to participants in *Sharing Shalom* who are interested in learning more about some of the topics that you discussed.

On Christianity and Judaism:

Carmody, Denise Lardner and John Tully Carmody. *Christianity: An Introduction.* Belmont, CA: Wadsworth Publishing Co., 1995.
    In a mere 250 pages, this volume overviews Christian theology and history, being particularly sensitive to incorporating Eastern Orthodox, Protestant and Roman Catholic perspectives.

Cohn, Emil Bernhard. *This Immortal People: A Short History of the Jewish People.* Translated with prologue and epilogue by Hayim Perelmuter. New York/Mahwah, NJ: Paulist Press, 1985.
    This reprint of a work originally published in Germany in 1936 offers a sweepingly concise yet thorough outline of biblical and postbiblical Jewish history. It is a most accessible introduction to Jewish history to those not familiar with it.

Cunningham, Lawrence S. *The Catholic Faith: An Introduction.* New York/Mahwah, NJ: Paulist Press, 1987.
    This volume introduces Roman Catholicism as a faith community with a defining sacramental character that leads to an ethical way of life.

Greenberg, Irving. *The Jewish Way: Living the Holidays.* New York: Summit Books, 1988.
    Greenberg, an Orthodox rabbi and important modern thinker, offers wonderful insights into the Jewish experience and faith tradition through this exploration of Jewish holy days and festivals.

113

Kushner, Harold. *To Life! A Celebration of Jewish Thinking and Being.* Boston: Little, Brown and Co., 1993.
> The Conservative rabbi and popular author of *When Bad Things Happen to Good People* offers here a personal and appealing overview of Jewish spirituality and perspectives on life.

Magida, Arthur J., ed. *How to Be a Perfect Stranger: A Guide to Etiquette in Other People's Religious Ceremonies.* 2 vols. Woodstock, VT: Jewish Lights Publishing, 1996–97.
> These volumes outline the history and beliefs, basic worship service, religious calendar, life-cycle events and home celebrations of religious groups with members exceeding fifty thousand. Research was conducted through a questionnaire which was in almost all cases completed by the national office of the religion or denomination. Both volumes include a helpful glossary and calendar of religious holidays and festivals.

On Relations between Jews and Christians:

Cunningham, Philip A. *Education for Shalom: Religion Textbooks and the Enhancement of the Catholic and Jewish Relationship.* Collegeville, MN: The Liturgical Press, 1995.
> While assessing the presentation of Jews and Judaism in current Catholic religious education textbooks, this work presents a useful synopsis of the origins and contents of Christian anti-Jewish teaching and of the Catholic Church's modern renunciation of it. Recommendations for teachers and preachers are included that are useful for all Christian denominations.

Efroymson, David P., Eugene J. Fisher and Leon Klenicki, eds. *Within Context: Essays on Jews and Judaism in the New Testament.* Collegeville, MN: The Liturgical Press, 1993.
> This volume is a collection of essays on anti-Jewish rhetoric in the New Testament. They offer specific suggestions to preachers and teachers about using such texts. An opening essay examines Christian supersessionist theology, and treatments of the following topics: Second Temple Judaism, the Synoptic Gospels, the Gospel of John, Opposition to Jesus, the Death of Jesus, and Paul and the Law of Moses.

Flannery, Edward H. *The Anguish of the Jews: Twenty-Three Centuries of Antisemitism.* New York/Mahwah, NJ: Paulist Press/Stimulus Books, 1985.
> Written by a Catholic priest, this is now a classic presentation on the troubled

relationship between Judaism and Christianity from biblical times to the present. This is an especially important work for Christians, who in the author's words, have tended to rip out of their history books the pages that Jews have memorized.

Klenicki, Leon and Geoffrey Wigoder, eds. *A Dictionary of the Jewish-Christian Dialogue.* New York/ Mahwah, NJ: Paulist Press/Stimulus Books, 1984.
The editors have assembled in this volume pairs of very short essays, each written by a Jew and a Christian, on key terms or figures in the Jewish and Christian experience. Among the thirty-four topics considered are afterlife, creation, covenant, faith, God, prayer, revelation and salvation.

Saperstein, Marc. *Moments of Crisis in Jewish-Christian Relations.* London: SCM Press and Philadelphia: Trinity Press, 1992.
The author, a Reform rabbi and professor, examines the history of the church and the synagogue, focusing on four especially crucial periods: the Roman world, the late Middle Ages, the Reformation and the Holocaust. A concluding essay reflects on future prospects.

Talmage, F. E. *Disputation and Dialogue: Readings in the Jewish-Christian Encounter.* New York: KTAV Publishing House and Anti-Defamation League of B'nai B'rith, 1975.
For those who would like to read primary source materials on themes that Christians and Jews have argued about for centuries, such as election, messiah, law and gospel, and the Land of Israel, this book provides a handy and revealing collection.

About the Contributors

NORMAN ABELSON has more than four decades of direct involvement with communications as a journalist, press secretary, Washington lobbyist and researcher, and teacher. He offers commentaries for National Public Radio stations WBUR-FM in Boston and WEVO-FM in Concord. He is a member of the Jewish Christian Interfaith Partnership of New Hampshire and of the Board of Directors of the Shalom Center.

DR. PHILIP A. CUNNINGHAM is professor of theology and director of the Ministry Institute at Notre Dame College in Manchester, New Hampshire. He is a member of the Jewish Christian Interfaith Partnership of New Hampshire and Codirector of the Shalom Center.

BRO. PAUL R. DEMERS, S.C., D.Min., is campus minister at Rivier College in Nashua, New Hampshire, and adjunct faculty member of the Ministry Institute at Notre Dame College. He is also a member of the Jewish Christian Interfaith Partnership of New Hampshire.

DR. JOEL KLEIN is an ordained Conservative rabbi and full-time psychotherapist in private practice in Manchester, New Hampshire. He is working on two book manuscripts concerning the origins of Judaism and Christianity and holistic medicine. He is also a member of the Board of Directors of the Shalom Center.

REV. LOUISE MANN is an Episcopal priest serving as associate rector of Christ Church in Exeter, New Hampshire. She is a member of the Jewish Christian Interfaith Partnership of New Hampshire and of the Board of Directors of the Shalom Center.

REV. DR. PHILIP J. MAYHER is pastor and teacher at the Congregational Church of Weston, Massachusetts (U.C.C.). He is an adjunct faculty member at Andover-Newton Theological School and a member of the Board of Directors of the Shalom Center.

CLAIRE G. METZGER has been the cantor at Congregation Adath Yeshurun in Manchester since June 1995. She graduated from the Hebrew Union College Jewish Institute of Religion, School of Sacred Music, in May of 1994 with a Master of Sacred Music degree and investiture as cantor.

JOAN PORO, a Roman Catholic, is pastoral associate at St. Joseph Cathedral in Manchester, New Hampshire. She holds a Master of Arts degree in theology from Notre Dame College and is a member of the Jewish Christian Interfaith Partnership of New Hampshire and of the Board of Directors of the Shalom Center.

DR. BARBARA ANNE RADTKE is associate professor of theology and Codirector of the Ministry Institute at Notre Dame College. She is also a member of the Jewish Christian Interfaith Partnership of New Hampshire and of the Board of Directors of the Shalom Center.

DAVID G. STAHL, D.M.D., is a Manchester native, a practicing dentist and an amateur musician. He has served as president of the Greater Manchester Jewish Federation, chairman of the New Hampshire unit of the American Jewish Committee and is the immediate past president of Congregation Adath Yeshurun in Manchester. He is also a member of the Jewish Christian Interfaith Partnership of New Hampshire.

RABBI ARTHUR F. STARR, D.D., a Reform rabbi, is spiritual leader of Congregation Adath Yeshurun in Manchester, New Hampshire, where he has served for twenty-five years. He is a member of the Jewish Christian Interfaith Partnership of New Hampshire and Codirector of the Shalom Center.

ELLEN ZUCKER is a marketing professional in the field of work and life issues and is active in educational and spiritual programs at Temple Beth Abraham in Nashua, New Hampshire. She holds a Bachelor of Jewish Studies degree from Scripps College in Claremont, CA. She is a member of the Jewish Christian Interfaith Partnership of New Hampshire.

What to Do Next

Joan Poro

By the end of our fourth session of *Sharing Shalom,* participants already were asking, "What happens next?" The small group facilitators decided that on the final night we would allow time at the end of the evening for a large group discussion of that concern. Both in the discussion and in the written evaluations, the majority of participants indicated keen interest in continuing the relationships they had begun to develop in these few weeks. Here are some common-sense principles to guide an ongoing journey toward greater *shalom:*

Stay in touch. If some of your participants have expressed interest in continuing in dialogue, provide them the opportunity. Invite all who are interested to a "reunion" to explore meaningful ways to continue dialogue.

Have a plan. Know what you hope to accomplish with this "reunion" meeting. Keep it simple. You want to further explore the question, "What happens next?"

Ask meaningful questions: *Why have you come back? What will keep you coming back?* Trust that the adults who come back will be motivated to take ownership in shaping the process, setting its pace, and naming what will be meaningful enough to keep them engaged.

Listen to the responses and list them on large sheets of newsprint.

Organize. What is the consensus? What are the priorities for dialogue topics?

Most of all, remember what first brought you together: the opportunity for interfaith dialogue.

Here is a plan that worked for us.

Two weeks after the final session of *Sharing Shalom* we sent an invitation to all the dialogue partners to a "reunion" to continue an informal dialogue about "What happens next?" Eighteen of our original group of thirty-one

118

accepted the invitation, while nearly everyone else asked to be kept informed of what came out of our meeting.

We greeted our friends with refreshments and name tags. The name tags were appreciated, as the participants had been divided into small dialogue groups for *Sharing Shalom* and many did not know people from other groups very well. We sat in a large circle and each had an opportunity to introduce oneself. Then in our introduction to the evening we noted that the group was forging a new path in local Jewish-Christian dialogue, moving beyond the six-week process of *Sharing Shalom*. The evening followed a plan with three movements:

Movement 1: Looking at the experience so far.

The participants were asked to gather with others they did not know well, in groups of two (no more than three) to discuss: *What were the positives about* Sharing Shalom *that you want to see continued? What was good about the six-week experience that is worth repeating or nurturing? In other words: Why have you come back?*

Reassembled in the circle, we shared our responses and listed them on a large sheet of newsprint.

Movement 2: Looking ahead—what happens next?

The list we had generated represented the hopes and goals that the partici-pants had brought into the meeting. We now asked: *How do we shape these features into a process for continuing dialogue?* This was the longest and most exciting movement, as ideas ranged from community service projects to edu-cational field trips to Bible study to methods for continuing dialogue. We listed all ideas on another sheet of newsprint.

Movement 3: Focus on dialogue.

It was at this point that we refocused the group on what brought us together in the first place: the opportunity for interfaith *dialogue*. Dialogue is not merely an impersonal discussion of ideas; nor is it a mere sharing of information. Although both of these elements may be present, dialogue involves a personal encounter with the other in which I am able to grow not only in my understand-ing and knowledge of the other, but also of myself and my own faith.

We brainstormed topics for dialogue and explored how best to prepare for dialogue sessions. The ideas, once again listed on newsprint, included:

◆ Reading short printed pieces on the dialogue subject (much as we did with *Sharing Shalom*).

♦ Inviting qualified speakers (one Jew and one Christian) to make brief presentations at the beginning of each meeting.

♦ Attending a talk or academic presentation as a group and meeting afterward for dialogue.

♦ Visit one another's places of worship either during services or at other times. (On a related note, clergy from the involved congregations might be invited to exchange pulpits one week so that other members of their communities might get to know about interfaith dialogue.)

Remembering that dialogue, then, is the glue that will keep us bonded, we can readily acknowledge and encourage the enthusiasm of some in our group to move beyond dialogue into community action. We talked about how this can be a natural, exciting (and optional) spin-off of continued dialogue. We discussed dialogue topics that might lead us in that direction, for example, teachings on economic justice.

The entire process took about an hour and a half. We concluded with a brief prayer led by the rabbi of the Temple where we were meeting.

We left with many choices yet to be made, but also with a sense of the limitless possibilities.

As Marc Gellman suggests in the reading in the sixth-session closing prayer of *Sharing Shalom,* our small group of Jews and Christians might begin to see ourselves as partners with God in bringing creation to completion. Coming together as people of faith, our continued dialogue may lead us to juxtapose our faiths and the reality of the world around us. What do we see and hear in our everyday lives that does not correspond to our understanding of the kingdom of God? What do we feel called to do about it?

"What happens next" is indeed a journey of the heart. God knows where it will take us. It is up to us to discover and to follow God's will for us, Christians and Jews together.

John Rousmaniere, *A Bridge to Dialogue: The Story of Jewish-Christian Relations;* edited by James A. Carpenter and Leon Klenicki (A Stimulus Book, 1991).

Michael E. Lodahl, *Shekhinah/Spirit* (A Stimulus Book, 1992).

George M. Smiga, *Pain and Polemic: Anti-Judaism in the Gospels* (A Stimulus Book, 1992).

Eugene J. Fisher, editor, *Interwoven Destinies: Jews and Christians Through the Ages* (A Stimulus Book, 1993).

Anthony Kenny, *Catholics, Jews and the State of Israel* (A Stimulus Book, 1993).

Eugene J. Fisher, editor, *Visions of the Other: Jewish and Christian Theologians Assess the Dialogue* (A Stimulus Book, 1995).

Vincent Martin, *A House Divided: The Parting of the Ways Between Synagogue and Church* (A Stimulus Book, 1995).

Leon Klenicki and Geoffrey Wigoder, editors, *A Dictionary of the Jewish-Christian Dialogue* (Expanded Edition), (A Stimulus Book, 1995).

Frank B. Eakin, Jr., *What Price Prejudice?* (A Stimulus Book, 1998).

STIMULUS BOOKS are developed by Stimulus Foundation, a not-for-profit organization, and are published by Paulist Press. The Foundation wishes to further the publication of scholarly books on Jewish and Christian topics that are of importance to Judaism and Christianity.

Stimulus Foundation was established by an erstwhile refugee from Nazi Germany who intends to contribute with these publications to the improvement of communication between Jews and Christians.

Books for publication in this Series will be selected by a committee of the Foundation, and offers of manuscripts and works in progress should be addressed to:

Stimulus Foundation
c/o Paulist Press
997 Macarthur Boulevard
Mahwah, N.J. 07430